Bob Roberts provides the road map to moving the local church from form to function, from worship to witness, from singing to soul winning, from globalization to glocalization. If you desire to learn how to put your faith and feet together for effective, changed lives, *Transformation* is for you.

James O. Davis, cofounder/president/CEO,
Global Pastors Network, Orlando, Florida

Don't tell Pastor Bob Roberts that Christian churches cannot walk boldly and openly into other closed and sometimes dangerous cultures and build relationships that will make a kingdom impact, for he has done it! This book will inspire and challenge anyone who reads it to a new dimension of involvement in the Great Commission.

Jerry Rankin, president, International Mission Board, SBC

Bob Roberts, his family, and his church are on a radical journey, discovering the substance that trumps style. This book is about that journey and the process. This is a stimulating, challenging, and important book for pastors or church leaders who want to lead whole congregations from talk and the illusion of changing the world to being agents of its transformation, inside and out.

Ray Bakke, founder of International Urban Associates

Bob Roberts, as his name suggests, is two times larger than life — a man that a single name cannot contain. When you're too big for just Texas, as is the case for Bob, then you are a man of incredible stature. He will not rest until the entire world has heard the Good News of his Savior Jesus Christ. I would gladly take any hill with Bob beside me.

Neil Cole, author of *Organic Church: Growing Faith Where Life Happens, Cultivating a Life for God*, founding leader of Awakening Chapels and director of Church Multiplication Associates

Bob Roberts is part of a new breed of Christian leaders who build big churches and then build leaders to multiply them so that they serve not hundreds but thousands. He is squared-jawed, muscular, and hyper-energetic, the kind of guy you would want to follow into war or up a mountain face. His passion is building the teams that build churches and expanding the kingdom. This book tells how.

Bob Buford, founder of Leadership Network, the Drucker Foundation for Non-Profit Management, and author of *Halftime*

What happens when you combine in one person boundless energy, deep and radical faith, native intelligence, courage to take huge risks, an activist passion to change the world, and a truly global vision? You get Bob Roberts — a guy with a heart the size of Texas. I benefit on many levels whenever I am under the influence of this unique brother in Christ. I am thrilled his influence will spread through this exciting, challenging, and transformative book.

Brian McLaren, pastor (crcc.org) and author
(anewkindofchristian.com)

In spite of what some think, we don't change how we do church to make people mad. At the heart of Christianity is the transformation of the Christian's heart (2 Cor. 3:18). And we change how we do church to facilitate this kind of deep transformation in the lives of our people. While Bob covers much more than this, he covers this, and we need a strong dose of it.

Aubrey Malphurs, president of the Malphurs Group
and professor at Dallas Seminary

Bold brother Bob has caught a glimpse of the King and his Kingdom that is big enough to help us all make sense of our lives and ministries. His refreshing passion for the whole gospel to be brought to the whole world is a timely treasure.

Mark Driscoll, pastor of Mars Hill Church
and president of the Acts 29 Network

Bob Roberts combines the passion of a practitioner with a keen mind and passion for missional engagement. As I read this book, I was both challenged and encouraged toward a deeper commitment to transformation and ministry, in my own life and through my church.

Ed Stetzer, author of *Planting New Churches
in a Postmodern Age*

From the moment Bob discovered the Kingdom of God and transformation everything came together for him. This compelling account unpacks an inspiring story of Bob's journey to and from his discovery, drawing out the principles and lasting lessons for Christians and churches in the US and around the world that are both transforming and transformational.

Luis Bush, Transform World Connections International Facilitator

What Bob offers in this book is far more valuable than a program or package; it is, rather, a story of success that emerges from the ashes of personal brokenness. If true revival is known by its comprehensive embrace of cities and nations, it begins with the transformation of the individual heart.

George Otis Jr., CEO, The Sentinel Group

Transformation is an American book that other nations will applaud. It's a bridge to some answers that have been eluding us. It clearly outlines what has gone wrong with the American church and frames a future hope that is missional, transformational, oriented around convergence, pilgrimage, and a close walk with our Creator.

Andrew Jones Boaz, director of Boaz Project
(http://tallskinnykiwi.com)

TRANSFORM*ATION*

Discipleship that Turns Lives,
Churches, and the World
Upside Down

BOB ROBERTS JR.

 ZONDERVAN®

ZONDERVAN.com/
AUTHORTRACKER
follow your favorite authors

LEADERSHIP ✖ NETWORK®

ZONDERVAN

Transformation
Copyright © 2006 by Bob Roberts Jr.

This title is also available as a Zondervan ebook.
Visit www.zondervan.com/ebooks.

This title is also available in a Zondervan audio edition.
Visit www.zondervan.fm.

Requests for information should be addressed to:

Zondervan, *Grand Rapids, Michigan* 49530

This edition: ISBN 978-0-310-32608-3 (softcover)

The Library of Congress has catalogued the earlier edition as follows:

Roberts, Bob, 1958–
    Transformation : how glocal churches transform lives and the world / Bob Roberts, Jr.
      p. cm.
    Includes bibliographical references and index.
    ISBN 978-0-310-26717-1
    1. Church development, New. I. Title.
  BV652.24.R63 2005
  262'.001'7 — dc22   2005013739

Interior design: Ruth Bandstra

Printed in the United States of America

10 11 12 13 14 15 /DCI/ 23 22 21 20 19 18 17 16 15 14 13 12 11 10 9 8 7 6 5 4 3 2 1

*To my biggest hero — the person who has emulated most what
I have come to believe and write about —
my mom — Gaye Roberts.*

*To my greatest hope, the future church —
children of the staff at NorthWood: Ben, Jill, Ti, Paige,
Andrew, Ben, Addie, Kara, Allison, Lexi, Corbin, Landry,
Erin, Jenna, Jamie P., Jamie R., Lyndsey, Michelle, Derek,
Jordon R., Lauren, Jordon D., Morgan, Mason, Caitlin,
Jordan F., Amber, Ashlee, Parker, Jordan W.*

CONTENTS

ACKNOWLEDGMENTS

T here are so many people that have made possible the publishing of this book. Thanks to Nikki, Ben, Jill, and Ti for allowing me as your husband and father to explore and risk on this life pilgrimage — all the while pulling you along and now watching you run ahead. Thanks to NorthWood for your desire to not "do" church or "have" church but to "be" the church beyond a Sunday event. Thanks to Johnnie, Mike, Jordon, Randy, Matt, Mark, Omar, Cristian, Dave, Lance, Ross, Debbie, Angela, Karyn, Dustin, Suzanne, Susan, Diana, Karen, Sheila, Ann, Kay, Delores, Debby, Bill, Al — you are the world's greatest staff! Phuc, Andy, Kirk, Dennis and Danielle, Glenn, Sara — you have all been and continue to be a part of all this.

Thanks to all the NorthWood church plants and GlocalNet churches that are learning together to do community development, church multiplication, and nation building. What a joy to see great-great-granddaughter churches planted here in the States. What a joy to trek the globe with my young brothers engaging the infrastructures of Afghanistan, Egypt, Indonesia, Vietnam, many other nations and more to come. I love you, Bloye, Lightsey, Pittman, Gomez, Vassar, Harris, Brunner, Walker, Carmack, Land, Edmondson, Ford, Coloñ, Christopherson, Blocker, Sharp, Ruppe, Howard, McGlohon, and Shadrack.

Thanks to Bob Buford, Linda Stanley, and Dave Travis for persistently encouraging me and challenging me to move far beyond anything I had dreamed possible. You believed in me and invested in me — and we got an awesome return.

Thanks to Chris Grant; had I not met you, this book may not be here. Thanks also to Mary Ann Lackland; had I not met you, this book might not be legible! Thanks as well to Paul Engle and Zondervan—you're the best.

Thanks to Rick Warren—you began my journey of how to communicate to our culture in relevant ways and to grow our church. Thanks to Thom Wolf and Carol Davis—you taught me how to grow "the" church and modeled "glocal" for me. Thanks to Len Sweet—you made me think. Thanks to John Maxwell—you taught me leadership.

Thanks to Bobb Biehl, Leighton Ford, Roy Fish, and E. B. Brooks; for many years you have consistently encouraged, challenged, and shaped me. How different my life would have been had I not known you. Thanks to Dietrich Bonhoeffer, Richard Foster, Dallas Willard, E. Stanley Jones, Leo Tolstoy—you helped me understand the kingdom of God.

Thanks to Phuc and Thao, Manuel, Pukar, Vince, Alain, and Nghi; you have brought the world into my home on a daily basis.

Part One

SURVIVAL QUESTIONS FOR THE CHURCH:

What Would Your Church Be Like If ...?

What would it look like for your church to turn the world upside down?

What would it be like for people to find Christ because of hundreds of new Christians' testimonies of radical transformation?

What would it be like to celebrate what God is doing in all the Church, Capital C?

What would it be like to see the entire body mobilized to touch people everywhere in all dimensions and not a church based on a single charismatic leader?

If someone were to have asked me nineteen years ago when I started NorthWood Church whether our church today is what I always dreamed it would be like, I would have answered with a resounding, "No!" I assumed by now instead of 2,000 in attendance, we'd have 20,000 attending the most creative service around. Ours was the epitome of an emerging, fast-growing contemporary church. We grew to a membership of 500 and purchased a new facility in only four years. In a two-month period, we bought forty-five acres, relocated to a shopping center, and everything fell apart. But at the same time, everything came together. I discovered things I had never heard or understood. I discovered the kingdom of God and transformation. From there, God began to change my priorities and transform NorthWood. I had to see my own dreams crash to see God and what he wanted.

But never in a million years would I have dreamed we would have planted eighty churches, helped to start GlocalNet[1] (an informal network where we help church planters develop their own church-planting networks), and impacted a nation in significant ways. It came out of brokenness and changed my whole perception of what church was and what it really meant to follow Jesus. I began to realize many things about me and about the Western church in general:

- We have learned relevance and communication, but not transformation.
- We have learned purpose and functionality, but not essence and core DNA.
- We know so much of how, but so little of why.
- We want to change the world, and we become managers of organizations.
- We make people more religious, but no different spiritually or culturally.
- We know what we believe, but we cannot live it.
- We think we are respectable, but we have lost credibility.
- We have become mass media market, not a movement to shake the world.

Is this what I gave my life to? That's the question, isn't it? Christian leaders who signed on to change the world have instead become abandoned-mall managers as the rest of the world moves out into the new suburbia. Pastors were told, "Grow it big, and you'll change the world." So, we have grown the largest megachurches in Christian history. Only we did not anticipate that fewer people would be attending church today than in the past. Moreover, the latest research tells us most church attendees live their lives no differently from nonbelievers.[2] In other words, lost people live the same as many believers do; lost people just don't deny how they live. Still, we draw weekend crowds to give us the carefully orchestrated illusion that we are making an impact, but we are not seeing people's lives and our communities truly transformed.

It's not that we don't want to change the world. We do, but we don't know how. More importantly, we haven't deliberately thought through the question of "Why?" Some of us are content to appease our consciences by hiring personnel to change the world for us. However, the undeniable reality that fewer people in our Western society are attending church today than ever before is creating a healthy unrest among many believers and church leaders. Something is wrong.

Don't misunderstand—there is a lot to celebrate. The church is at its strongest ever financially, educationally, and politically, even though some would readily disagree on those points. Yet, my fear is that it has become institutionalized and denominationalized to the point where the primary things we ask of people is their money, attendance, and a few hours every quarter to help with a Sunday school project. Tragically, entire denominations and institutions continue to fight old battles (of which most laypeople no longer see the relevance) instead of funneling the trillions of dollars flowing through their systems toward the one goal of making a significant difference in our world. We don't make a difference because the gospel has not made us different as God intended it to do. We are just more religious. We are more worried that our church is not growing than the fact that we are not growing in our walk with God.

For all that has been lost in the Western church today, there is hope. There has never been a greater opportunity to see the transformation of people, society, and the world, but it will mean a radical redefinition of following Christ and impacting the world. "Glocal" churches create disciples who, transformed by the Holy Spirit, are infiltrating today's culture on a global and local scale with the undeniable message of a changed life.

I am finding hope—not in the expression of the Western church but in what God is doing around the world and in the emerging church. If you read the West's accounts of what the church will look like in the future, it is always the fringe expressions of the emerging youth culture and churches. They may have been the indicator of the past. However, they are not the indicator of the future. The emerging church in China, the Middle East, India, and other developing nations give us more clues to the future of the church than any Western expression. I'm learning more about how to do church from the East than I am from the West!

The church has been stripped of its power and influence in the West today, not because it has lost its wealth and position in society —it hasn't—but because the church has lost its credibility. On the whole, we can hardly change ourselves, much less the world. We cannot consistently live the message we herald to the world, but never have we been more effective at religious marketing of products that help us appear as if we are living it. As a result, the growing perception is that the church is religious but not spiritual. It has style but not enough substance.

That's why I believe the basis of this transformation is a combination of the early church's example in Acts with what is emerging in the Eastern church. It is in stark contrast to the Western approach to discipleship, namely, the transfer of information through curricula. This approach results in educated converts who may grow churches, not necessarily radically transformed disciples who will change the world.

Most people do not make the journey of transformation because somehow they just cannot begin making a difference locally and globally (i.e., glocally). If transformation stops after conversion, they weren't converted. If it stops after instruction, according to Paul they get puffed up. They may be able to answer all kinds of Bible questions, understand theology, and even write inspirational books, but they'll never know Christ on an intimate level that leads to true transformation. Only the person who converges the two—what they learn on a consistent daily basis with their lifestyle—has any hope of transformation.

My own transformation came with the discovery of the kingdom of God—which is far more than a widget machine spitting out parts. We jump into it like a river, holding fast to Christ on an unpredictable adventure. The world has some hard questions for the church about the transformation that is supposed to have taken place inside us—questions we must address. Where do we begin? Grab your inner tube and join me in this journey of transformation: living beyond ourselves and our own four walls.

ONE

HOW DO WE FIND OUR VOICE AGAIN?

I was speaking in Australia and was on my way from Sydney to Perth. On the overnight flight, I got up to stretch my legs in the back of the plane. A young flight attendant began making polite small talk as she prepared the drink cart, asking me where I was from, where I was going, and what I did for a living. I often hesitate to tell people I'm a pastor—our reputation is not exactly well received. That day, however, I just let it go. "I'm a pastor," I began. "I'm here to speak at some seminaries and colleges in Australia about how to start churches." What a great opener for an evangelism experience! Right! Only she didn't seem the least intrigued.

"Good luck. You won't get much of an audience here," she said nonchalantly. "I think you'll find it's quite different than what you see in America. No offense, just the way it is."

"None taken," I offered. Now I was the one intrigued. "So what's the deal? Is God just not part of the equation of life? What do most Australians think of him?"

She didn't hesitate. "It isn't that I'm angry with God or don't believe in him. He's just not a player, if you will."

Granted, she maintained her friendly flight attendant demeanor, but her matter-of-fact response to the topic at hand still threw me. "So help me understand this," I probed. "Have you been hurt in the past by the church somehow?"

"No," she smiled, undeterred. "My granny goes to church. As a matter of fact, I had a friend who had an awesome tragedy. The way the church stepped in and helped out was incredible. No questions asked."

I retraced our steps. "But you believe in God?"

"Of course. You'd have to be an idiot *not* to believe. I'm very spiritual, as are most of my friends; I'm just not religious."

"How do you get in touch with your spirituality?" Great, there's a token pastor-type question. She took it in stride, however, as she continued loading her cart.

"I walk in the bush, or take a long walk on the beach, or visit with my mates for a long time."

"What would make you want God or pursue him in your life?" *What was this bloke getting at?* she must have wondered.

She paused for a moment before responding, "I can't answer that. I'm just perfectly happy without him."

"So not angry, bitter, or resentful—just indifferent?" I offered once more.

"That's it," she concluded.

That *was* it. Tragically, Christianity (as she understood it) had nothing to offer this young woman. How can that be? Does the gospel have the ability to reach happy people who "have it all"? Or is it just a crisis decision? I knew Jesus spoke to deep levels of truth and meaning beyond a crisis, but I was having a difficult time convincing her of that. Is the gospel powerful enough to *be enough* in and of itself, or does someone have to respond only because they're hurting? How do we help people understand that they need God because he's God and that there's no true or ultimate meaning without him?

As I visited with her, I ached over the flaws in our understanding of what it is that we invite people to experience and our inability to engage the culture at a significant depth. Where is the church today speaking to justice and mercy? Where is the church today serving the poor and the hurting? Where is the church today serving as a prophet to society? Her view of the church was that it existed as an institution for itself—neither good nor bad, just irrelevant to her.

We cannot expect to help people understand there is value to following God and a depth of life that comes no other way if we don't deal with issues at this level. We would have nothing different to offer them from the Buddhists, Hindus, Muslims, animists, and other religions who merely beseech their gods in times of need for things they desire. When America was more "Christian" in its cultural moorings, it wasn't necessary to understand apologetics. Thinking about the deep issues regarding the existence of God was not as prevalent then; now that has all changed.

Thinking and apologetics are no longer options reserved for the serious student of evangelism; they are basics for every believer now.

When the church began to institutionalize and focus on gaining influence in political arenas and amassing wealth and respectability in global affairs, it lost its mooring—the central message of hope and healing that will transform individuals and cultures. The church became a regimented system, corralling its constituents into programs—and yet not without results. Megachurches exploded. Church networks grew. Something was happening—and as long as the numbers grew, we self-validated all the results. Instead of all our movement being God's work, we convinced ourselves of the opposite. We surmised all our feverish work must signify a movement of God.

I HAD TO GO HALFWAY AROUND THE WORLD TO FIND IT

How did this colossal mistake happen? Somewhere along the way, we became lost. I didn't even realize how lost I was until I saw what the church was really supposed to look like. At first, I didn't even recognize it; then I wanted to rationalize it. I had to go halfway around the world to find it—in the persecuted underground house church in Asia. I had heard the stories and statistics, but I had never met anyone face to face. For the first time, I found people who were living a *Divine Conspiracy*,[1] as Dallas Willard would say. They were nothing like me. They were nothing like any believers I had ever met — not even Willard! Not just culturally, but spiritually they blew me away. Sure, their theology is fuzzy. Some don't even have whole parts of the Bible, only perhaps an entire book or a few passages. But they know God at a depth I never had nor knew anyone else who had.

Worship takes on a completely new expression on the other side of the world. No sound systems, no calculated transitions, just sweaty believers crammed together into small rooms, weeping as the Holy Spirit oozes out among them, as I never before experienced. I don't know if they are charismatic or not (all I knew was it wasn't my tongue), but it doesn't matter. No one is getting rich, and no one is fighting for control or position. If there is a favored position, it is the privilege of being the first to die. Living on the edge as they do leaves little room for insincerity or self-promotion. These people are living what I grew up hearing the church should be.

Through small, indigenous, underground house church networks, these churches are transforming lives and their cultures. They cannot be stopped. There are too many of them, and they are spreading everywhere, every day. Here's a shocker: Laypeople start these movements, not just those "called" to full-time vocational ministry. Their church planting is the result of transformed lives and not the result of a grand strategy, even though the strategy is grand.

The differences are striking and so are the results — so much so that in spite of holding so many degrees and an earned doctorate, I've learned more about how to do church from outside America than I ever did inside America. I firmly believe that in order to find the real church, one has to get on a plane and fly west at least twelve hours over the Pacific. And then, one won't find it in a church building — it will be in a neighborhood. Don't go looking for it on Sunday, but seek it early in the morning or late at night as people quietly come in singles and pairs in order to not draw attention to themselves.

The farther west I fly, the more the food doesn't agree with me and my body is dirty and aching, but my soul gets free and clean. When I return home, I grow cleaner on the outside and the amenities of my culture pace alongside my physical comfort, but spiritually, the dirt of a polluted church clings to my soul.

The well-intentioned theme of today's missiological literature is about how the doors are opening for the West to rush in and "give them what we have and what we know." Do we really want to give them Western Christianity? Are we so proud of what we are producing that we are ready to export it to the nations?

Frankly, we have more need of them than they have of us. My greatest fear for the church in Asia is the Americans who want to go and "help." How arrogant we are to think that we must rush our missionaries over to closed parts of the world to tell them how to "do church."

God, save them from us, and let them help us become more of who they are!

WEST LEARNS FROM THE EAST

Many of the things we do to grow the church may even unintentionally keep it from growing as large as it could and affecting the culture as strongly as it should.

It's time for the American church to go back to school. In the West, we value visible results, which inevitably lead to pragmatism and systems. We hire personnel and superstar preachers and leaders to do the job. We challenge people to sacrifice money to build bigger buildings so we can build a big church. And we do. But in the end, we have little if any cultural impact.

In the East, it's just the opposite: They value obedience, which comes from passion and love. Results are not seen in baptisms but are demonstrated in obedience and the courage to follow Christ. Fluidity is the key to their success—things change too fast in a church culture where people in leadership positions can be arrested. Therefore, the movement's progress is not tied to programs or processes, but it is linked to people: trained individuals who carry on the essence of the church in their character.

Everyone has to serve in this community for it to work, and the pastor is the chief example of how to handle faith in difficult circumstances. They challenge people to have courage, and they sacrifice their lives, not just their money. We in the American church write about a longing for what a life of faith should be; in the East, this is their reality.

They have no big churches, only thousands of little churches decentralized into every neighborhood. And they are having a huge cultural impact. Can we just pass this off as an anomaly? Certainly not. True, we can give the rest of the church lessons on how to grow a single church big and process its members, but what church in America (mine included) can claim to know and practice how to radically change the culture? (Fighting the culture with political maneuvering and scheming notwithstanding, we've just about lost our credibility with that strategy.)

Before we can figure out where we go from here, we have to realize how deep into the woods we've wandered. In other words, we have to understand how we became lost in order to find our way back.

HOW DID THIS HAPPEN?

We Have Become Lost in Modernity

We thought that the hallmarks of modernity—individuality, reason, science, and optimism—would build the church like never before. And it did grow and lives were changed. In American culture, production, momentum, and results reign supreme. However, as Western pragmatists, we too often believed that as long as we could produce results, we didn't need to examine the results we were getting.

Meanwhile, in trying to mimic the best our culture had to offer, the church discovered it could no longer separate itself from it. In time we became one. Churches, governments, and corporations all operated on the same principles with different products. American culture and the American church merged so closely they became virtually indistinguishable. In that period, a tragic irony took place. The church took on more of the culture than the culture took on the church. In turn, the church learned how to use the tools of the culture to build its own empire.

We Have Become Lost in Consumerism

To a large degree, growing churches today must appeal to the consumer mindset in terms of what services we are providing to meet our people's needs and how well we can entertain them. In other words, we have somehow turned the church into the ultimate "religious consumer" in order to make the gospel palatable to all. We assume the more needs we can meet through extensive programming, the healthier our people will be. Sadly, when we equate the size of our church with the level of our people's spirituality, we have miscalculated our own level of success.

In reality, most churched people think their sacrifice and service to God is their semifaithful attendance and occasional token offering. *That* is spirituality! To say that size is the only way to measure spiritual health is to take size out of context. Consider how cancerous tumors grow from healthy cells multiplying out of control—large in size, but disastrous to human health.

We Have Become Lost in Success

Though churches are growing by hundreds and thousands annually, there must be more to the success of a church than how many show up on Sunday. I often ask myself, our staff, and congregation, "Beyond the mega-obsession with large parcels of land, big buildings, and impressive budgets, what have we really accomplished?" I remind them that if people aren't truly transformed because of all we are doing, nothing in our communities, our country, and our world will be transformed. Do we best see the measure of transformation primarily in the pew or in the community? Consumerism and megamania would point to the pew, while the true measure of the impact of the gospel in the life of a church is not solely attendance. If community transformation became the measure of our success, how would our churches and our communities look different? How would we look different?

The question is not should churches grow, but why should they grow?

In the early days of my ministry, I never stopped to ask why, only how. The key was to find a guru, follow that person's steps, and watch the church and your influence grow exponentially. I think most leaders define significance and success to some degree in comparison to their peers. We have seen new paradigms of ministry; we need to see new paradigms of success and significance.

By this time, assuming you've stuck with me so far, you may think I despise all that is large in the American church. Not at all. I'm not saying we shouldn't be concerned about measurable indicators such as attendance and baptisms. Any church that is not growing should be concerned and seek to know why it is not growing. The church where I pastor has forty-five acres. We have a master plan to handle thousands of people, and we are getting close to our goals. However, I have often told our church that the justification for our being significant is not merely the fact that many people attend our church. A church is not significant and doing what God wants just because many people fill their rolls.

There should be far more that defines a church's success than putting on a good show on Sunday. When people say the name of your church and the church you attend or in which you serve, what do they think? May it be that we love God with all our beings and are trying to live transparent lives of integrity. May they see us giving out all that we have and all that we are.

We Have Become Lost in Megamania

Throughout history we've had megachurches; they are not new, just more prevalent. They have the ability to be incredible, unique blessings to the rest of the body—as long as they have deep roots and are centered on Christ. Being centered on Christ isn't just part of our statement of faith, but a recognized practice of that fact to which the world and community of nonbelievers can attest. For a tree to grow into significance, it has to develop deep roots. Many times, we impatiently settle for a good-sized bush that may appear to have the fortitude of a tree. However, when the winds blow, it easily snaps. If I selfishly look at ministry in terms of me, mine, and what I can see in my time, then roots don't seem to matter as much. We're tempted to "build it big and forget about sinking deep." However, if I look at ministry as something that will grow beyond me, my time, and my four walls, then I have to give equal attention to the roots.

What if, instead of looking at their peers, Christian leaders today looked at history, specifically the history of the early church? The result would be accountability to living at a higher level. Leaders and laypeople would live at an elevated level. Affirmation would not be nearly as important in their personal lives as sheer determination to get it done.

We Have Lost the Spirit to Industrialization

When I study the Great Awakenings in America, I'm intrigued by the fact that the surge of evangelism came not because of a massive crusade but through small, rural churches that touched their communities. In other words, evangelism was the result of an awakened church. Today, we practice evangelism without an awakened church. It's heartbreaking to consider how some have determined to grow big churches and do great evangelism but to do it totally apart from the awakening power of the Holy Spirit. We have immobilized ourselves to great preaching, relevant music, and dynamic programs so that we are convinced we no longer have to rely or depend on the Holy Spirit as we once did.

The Western church, at first blessed but then plagued with modernity, industrialization, and pragmatism, has "programmed" everything in the Christian life. We have segmented and compartmentalized the different dimensions of the church and thereby failed to understand its function in terms of the whole. We've taken church community life and made a program and system out of everything, from starting a Sunday school class or a small group. Purchasing the program package at a conference may lead some to think it guarantees any church in any setting impressive results. Don't many large churches, denominations, and parachurch groups promise success?

However, fads, styles, methods, and trends all come and go with the years as the church moves throughout time. Yet one thing has remained constant throughout Scripture and all of church history to this very moment—what Jesus taught as the kingdom of God. The obsession of the church must become the obtainment of the kingdom of God. Without it, we are lost. Without it, we are ineffective. Without it, we have no hope of a future and no hope for anyone else. Without it, there is no purpose for the existence of the church—no matter how slick your purpose statement is.

What is the kingdom of God? What does it look like? It's not an idea or an impotent notion, but it's something to live out in our everyday existence. It's a consistent theme throughout the Bible, and it is our reality as believers. It's a whole world perspective on what God is up to in the world today. The kingdom of God is not a widget machine—bigger, better, faster. It isn't impersonal, processed, and programmed. Instead, there is a divine flow to the kingdom that goes beyond mere mechanical production of religious people and products. It is an invigorating, life-giving, and adventuresome river, flowing throughout the world and channeling people into its white-water rapids. Grab an inner tube and hang on!

We Have Lost Our Leadership from Great Souls to Great Stars

Because the church mimics and produces its "religious" version of everything the secular world offers, it's no wonder many pastors and religious leaders build platforms of religious superstar status. A powerful religious leader is defined by how well they preach to the masses, how well they entertain, and how much information they pass along. Someone is "called of God" not because of the way the person lives but because of the way the person speaks!

Many people say of their favorite Christian pastor or personality, "If only I could preach or sing like that person." "If only I was the leader he or she is." In the Western church, few are remarking about our current leadership style, "If only I could know Jesus as he or she does." Neither have I heard any of the performers say like Paul, "Imitate me."

We talk about the qualifications for ministry in terms of education, ordination, rules, and regulations. However, isn't the main qualification for ministry the ability for a person to say, "Imitate me"? Not that they are perfect, but they are willing to live their lives as examples for others. One of my goals is that before I die, people might be able to say of me as they did of Francis of Assisi or A. W. Tozer, "O to know God like he did!" Pastors know how they are perceived by the questions people ask of them.

> The greatest compliment that can be said of any pastor or person is, "That person is a man/woman of God."

As I began to understand how lost we were in this area, I realized God didn't call me to preach. Preaching is only a function; it's a tool. God called me to something much greater—he called me to the kingdom. Sadly, many pastors define how the kingdom of God is doing by how they are personally doing. If numbers are up, God must be pleased. If giving suffers a dip, the kingdom must suffer proportionately. The reality is that the kingdom is doing fine. It is bigger than any single church or religious organization. The kingdom is unstoppable.

The implications of this are huge. Worship isn't watching a couple of people preach and sing and lead; it's the entire body moving in harmony together. The message isn't merely the passing along of information; it's delivering the encouragement to continue to live out the truth of the Christian life.

Many young pastors and Christian leaders claim to feel "called to be leaders." In other words, the movement or vision isn't nearly as important as their leading a group of people. People who want to be leaders scare me—they're dangerous. Moses didn't want to be a leader, but Pharaoh did. David didn't want to be a leader, but Saul fought for his right to remain in power.

The call to the kingdom has never been about leadership. Leadership may use influence to operate, but kingdom leadership means accomplishing something for God that cannot be done alone. Others must be raised up to fulfill the mission. The best leaders are driven by a vision of something God has called them to accomplish and not a position in which to hold power.

Leaders who don't want to be leaders but are humble and passionate enough to die for a cause are the kind of people others will follow to hell and back. This is the kind of leader the persecuted church throughout Asia is raising up. But churches who value their position and focus on performance and production more than on a person's character and integrity will not find the strength necessary to carry the heavy loads for the leader of today.

Not long ago, I was with a pastor who left his particular ethnic background and went to a nation of a totally different race to start a church. This was a very closed and difficult country—it still is.

At the time, I wouldn't have given that guy any chance to do what God had put on his heart. He reminded me of a real Texan: fighting hell with a water pistol! However, fifteen years later, he meets in a public hall and has over 5,000 every weekend. But that's not the end of the story—he's heavily involved with community development to the degree that the national government quietly partners with him. Why? Because he gets results! He has started three hundred other churches in this nation and surrounding countries. He also trains his businessmen who travel internationally in difficult places to plant house churches.

I want to be like him! A megachurch with a megafocus! He cracks me up—he's so filled with joy. Because I love being around him, one day I insisted that he take a run with me every morning for an hour—not something he was used to doing. Later, as we were worshiping with a small group of people, he wouldn't leave me alone until I danced "in the Spirit" with him—not something I'm real used to doing! It was so "Holy Ghastly" that no one encouraged a repeat performance!

We Have Become Lost in the Culture and Have Lost Our Voice

Local churches are intended to be God's expression of his kingdom in given communities. However, are they expressions of God today? We have church buildings all across North America, yet the church is viewed as irrelevant and out of touch—not making a difference. Worse yet, as my conversation with my Australian friend reminded me, we are not bringing any value or substance to society's ongoing conversation regarding what life is all about. People refer to their churches, their traditions, and their styles to formulate their likes and dislikes.

Even in the contemporary church today (of which I consider myself a part), we speak of contemporary and innovative issues in terms of style, format, and schedule rather than substance. For example, we spend a tremendous amount of energy trying to determine whether more people will come to a 9:30 service or an 11:00 service and whether we should have a praise team or acoustic set. However, are we as concerned with the message we have to offer them? We have learned to communicate in a relevant manner, but do we know our message?

Cultural forms of communication should and must always be relevant and speak the language of those whom we are addressing. But in trying to mirror the American culture's style, our message waned and we ceased to be the guiding conscience of the culture. We lost our voice. The message of the gospel is exceedingly powerful. How do we find our voice again?

Rick McKinley, who just wrote *Jesus in the Margins*,[2] is an incredibly refreshing young voice pastoring in Portland, Oregon. One day he told me how he started his church, which has grown significantly and is doing a lot of good work planting churches. Rick said that for the first few months, all he preached was "repentance" in order to experience God's kingdom. As a result, his church has reached hundreds of postmoderns and is making a huge impact in Portland. The message built a base to do what he's doing today.

We Have Lost Our Mission to Bureaucracies and Denominations

Institutions have grown so bureaucratic that many churches are now the primary funding sources for their own institutional missions that ironically often have little to do with those same local churches. "Missions," as defined today, is often the great buzzword to raise money for the institution, yet it has more to do with taxation for salaries and functions that serve the institution, not supporting the local churches that make all that happen. Many denominations have become special interest voices for the wealthy or the well-connected in religious power positions to push or promote agendas, as opposed to banding together corporately to turn the world upside down. What few and futile attempts are made are generally reactionary as opposed to intentional, missional, and proactive.

The voices of change to return us to our calling have been sounding for years but have been largely ignored and viewed as "fringe" elements. Even tenured consultants like Lyle Schaller and others have been challenging denominations to become more sensitive to serving the churches for which they are supposed to exist. I am convinced in my own denomination(s) (it's too splintered and fragmented to belong to any one denomination) the future belongs to the denomination or affinity group that raises a legitimate "missional" or, as I prefer, "kingdom" call.

We Have Lost Intimacy to Religion

The kingdom of God is bigger than any building, although most of us live our lives to build edifices in temporary settings. How foolish for the church, for Scripture tells us that we are to live for the eternal, not the temporary. Instead, it's possible to live our lives in such a way to demonstrate that the kingdom is far bigger than we are.

Understanding the personal dimension of the kingdom of God is life changing. Try starting, as I did, with reading slowly the Sermon on the Mount in Matthew 5. Have you ever read that slowly? (That's difficult enough since we are so desensitized to it.) But have you ever lived it? We've all read it—many have even preached a series on it. But the question is, "How do I live this stuff?" Oh, I understand the kingdom theologically. I've studied the textual explanations of the kingdom. I've read the scholars, the commentaries, and theologians and what they say that it means. What does it mean to live the kingdom of God personally inside? And then what does it mean to live it corporately as a church?

This seemed impossible to do when I first began to study it with intensity. Then I *really* began to be disturbed when I read where the disciples like John and Peter and even the apostle Paul said in effect, "Imitate me." In other words, "Live it like I'm living it." Some otherwise ordinary people *did* live out what Jesus taught—enough to lead by example.

Consider the qualifications for pastors, deacons, and those in Christian leadership in the New Testament. The majority of instructions deal more with intimacies such as a person's character and integrity than "religious" elements such as the theology and education of the person. I became convicted — not over the fact that I highly value education and theological training, but that I had underprioritized how it should influence a person on an intimate level.

Next, I stumbled onto Richard Foster's work. In the preface to his *Celebration of Discipline*, he questioned whether the Christian life and especially the Sermon on the Mount was truly real or merely a high idea, a noble notion, a wistful dream.[3] Prior to that point, it had been a high idea and a noble dream for me. Oh, I was a moral, good ol' Baptist. However, deep down my heart and my attitudes were no different from anyone else.

Next, I encountered Dallas Willard. I suddenly realized that our loss of intimacy to religion is a discipleship issue, pure and simple. The problem with evangelism (and any other tenet of Christianity) is not so much the sharing of our faith but the living of our faith.

We've become enamored with a Western university-model mindset originating from the monks in our Western university system. It's a didactic system — a transaction of information that is supposed to magically result in right living. How many of us have been told (and in turn told to others), "When you believe the right things, you'll start living right"? That's simply not true. Merely believing the right things *does not* ensure Christlike behavior.

So what was the key to the early church's success? They didn't have seminaries. There were few churches and fewer pastors. The majority couldn't even read. And there wasn't much of a New Testament Bible as we know it today. As a result, they did not practice merely education and information-based discipleship; it was a kind of discipleship resulting in radical behavioral transformation. We want to master the information; they longed to master the life.

In the West, we have allowed ourselves to separate believing the truth from its impacting the way that we live. This is not so in the Eastern churches. And until our beliefs, our lifestyle, our character, and our behavior come together, it will never, never work.

I even began to discover some of the great thinkers and theologians of our day have pressed this issue of the intimate versus the religious nature of our faith. Despite his role as a well-connected aristocrat with the Russian Orthodox Church, Tolstoy resonated with the intimacy of God more on the outskirts with the peasants than he did inside the religious institution. Tolstoy's understanding of the kingdom would unleash an incredible revolution in terms of impacting history and humanity, but the church distanced itself from the idea. Therefore, the church remained "religious" but not truly "different." Dietrich Bonhoeffer developed similar concepts regarding the practical "living out" of Jesus' message. It influenced the way he designed his seminary before going to prison during World War II.

Then I stumbled onto E. Stanley Jones (who, don't tell anyone, was a Methodist). He has become my teacher to a large degree because he didn't just talk about it; he lived it. And he just didn't live it; he practiced it in the context of being a missionary, a pastor, and a theologian.

One day I discovered Jones had written a biography of Gandhi, who was, believe it or not, one of the best practitioners of the personal nature of Jesus' message! Did you realize Gandhi spent an average of two hours a day meditating on the Gospels? By his own admission, Jesus' teachings in the Sermon on the Mount became the basis for a large portion of everything he did. That blew me away. No, he wasn't a Christian, nor did he claim to be. But the person of Jesus Christ and his Sermon on the Mount so moved him that it affected his life and work.

Something is tragically amiss when a man without Christ can change a nation and Christians who possess the Holy Spirit can't. According to Jones, Gandhi understood the cross as a lifestyle, as an act to be emulated, whereas most Christians understand the cross as a theology to be believed. The kingdom of God is a radical message meant to be lived out in radical lives, which then historically and culturally have radical results.

Gandhi did more with his half-truth in the understanding of the gospel and of the cross than most Christians do with a full grasp of the truth.

We are living in an age where the church's resources have never been greater. The thing the church lacks is not money, not education, not position, but modeling for the world to see the kingdom of God is alive, real, and true. People are not turned off by Jesus Christ. But they are turned off by us! They do not see the peace, hope, and integrity that they see in Jesus of Nazareth. Instead, they see hypocrites and religious bullies who can put on shows as good as the World Wrestling Entertainment!

Once I was visiting with a prominent young emerging leader of another country who is an atheist. After many discussions about God and the Bible over a period of months, I asked him, "If the Bible's promises and the meaning Jesus could bring to all our lives is true and you could know it for certain, would you follow him?" Without hesitation, this young atheist's response was, "Of course!" How will he see it if he can't see it in us?

KINGDOM IN, KINGDOM OUT

Understanding the kingdom as a river means getting in sync with the divine flow that says living and giving go hand in hand. This is a kingdom call that says integrity, character, and Jesus' principles of turning the other cheek are just as important as theological and historical issues. Although this idea does not exist in America today, it will one day soon. It will start small, struggling, but as it shapes the world and the lives of legitimate kingdom citizens, people will flock to it—tired of old fights and un-Christlike attitudes.

This divine flow of the kingdom of God is what I like to think of as "Kingdom In, Kingdom Out." It's inhaling and exhaling—do away with either and the oxygen supply is cut off, resulting in death.

Likewise, Jesus' Sermon on the Mount, the heart of kingdom living, focuses on being salt (Kingdom In) and light (Kingdom Out).

Salt and Light

Only two times in Matthew and very few times in the rest of the New Testament does Jesus say, "You are" something. Matthew 5:13 says, "You are the salt of the earth. But if the salt loses its saltiness, how can it be made salty again? It is no longer good for anything, except to be thrown out and trampled by men." Our light can illuminate only what we are—our character and integrity at the root of who we are.

I don't know any worship songs on salt. I know several songs on being the light, sending the light, shining the light. Light. Light. Light. However, according to Matthew 5, salt comes first. Salt is the basic flavor of our lives, much as it is the basic element of many foods. It's what attracts people to us and gives them a taste of what Jesus is like.

Salt comes first because we must be salt in our character before we can be effective as light. Even so, we are more attracted to light imagery because it speaks of proclamation and an eagerness to get out the message. However, light without salt is bland and not life-changing at all. In fact, it can be obnoxious and even dangerous. It's the difference between the warmth of a sunrise at daybreak versus the blinding glare of oncoming headlights on a dark road. Short-sighted churches shine light without first developing the saltiness within their people, and they may end up inadvertently blinding others to their message.

When we talk about salt and light we must remember it's not either–or; it's both–and. As the salt comes in, the light flows out. It happens in breaths, each breath building on the last breath. More salt, more light. However, focus only on salt without the output of light, and the salt cakes the walls of the church as salt encrusts the Dead Sea because the water has no natural outflow. It is the saltiest body of water on earth, but it cannot sustain life. The opposite is just as dangerous. Focus on light without salt and the result is a shallow, fad ministry or church with glitz and glitter. Where has the world been transformed as a result of glitz and glitter? Real change happens when the kingdom is found in the transformation of communities.

Robert Lewis, from Fellowship Bible Church in Little Rock, confronts us with a tough question for us to consider: If the church in a local community were gone, who besides her own adherents would miss it?[4] It's an uncomfortable question—but if we are salt *and* light, we will confess the gospel is not just for the group we have convinced inside our walls. It is a gospel that impacts communities and the world.

Whether They Follow or Not

You see, the kingdom means that we are committed to being salt and light whether the people we serve all become Christians or not. Today's notion of "us against them" Christianity would be foreign to the early church. It seems today that we primarily try to change the culture one of two ways. We compromise in order to get our way or we mobilize politically like the rest of the world and use their methods. Either way is the opposite of the method Jesus used. His method was his life. Evangelism wasn't a numbers promotion. His ministry wasn't a "come to church" event; it was a life event. Think about it—Jesus fed, healed, and served people in the communities whether they followed him or not.

Many will reject our message when we share our faith, but each encounter results in something positive inside of us. "Missions" is not just about proclamation—telling them. It's discipleship in action, and it actually often does more for our personal growth than it does for those with whom we seek to share.

QUESTIONS WORTH ASKING

Most in Christian leadership define their lives and ministry by a single church. What if instead it was defined by the church and the entire body of Christ? Wouldn't they move above self-centeredness and an accumulation mindset to focus more on mobilizing the entire body to move out into their communities and the world? Let your mind consider the possibilities:

- What would it be like to be a part of a church that exploded with growth, but it didn't merely benefit the single church that God was moving in?
- What would it be like for a pastor's chief job to be to mobilize the church to reach the ends of the world?
- What would it be like if every year 10 percent of a church membership left to become missionaries and church planters all over the world?

I have experienced some of these things, but not all of them. However, I know this: I will not be content until I do.

There are other implications for these questions and even more questions in need of answers—but that's what the rest of this book is about:

- realizing we've settled for buildings and audiences when God created us for the whole world
- getting in step with the early church and the kingdom—the ultimate ancient-future link
- being in touch locally and globally with the poor, the persecuted, and the underprivileged
- moving the church as a whole from numerical growth (if not decline) to exponential multiplying growth here and among the nations—from information to transformation, from believing it to living it.

The success mindset is moving off the radar screen of our present age as busters and millennials ask deeper questions of meaning and life. Stats go out the window when you give your life to something greater than organized religion or a me-centered personal relationship with Christ. It's no longer the increase in production but the transformed life that matters most to those who are willing to become the ultimate Christian survivalists and adventurers—thrill-seekers who are shooting the rapids. In this new era, faith is paramount and courage, indispensable.

QUESTIONS TO THINK ABOUT AND TALK ABOUT

1. What other things do you see that has caused the church to be lost?

2. How do you convince people they need Jesus when they have everything they perceive they need?

3. When you go to your church, do you think more about what you're going to get or what you're going to give? Why?

4. What do you think Jesus thinks of your church?

TWO

WHERE DOES THE CHURCH FIT?

My story is perhaps familiar to many people's experience in church life. When I went to the church where I currently serve as pastor, I had already served on a large church staff in another state. The pastor there would soon retire, and several people hinted to me that perhaps I would be the next senior pastor. To be honest, I became disillusioned as a young man in my twenties. During that time, I just assumed that Christian leaders lived what they taught or, I told myself, they wouldn't be in places of leadership. I was naïve, to say the least.

I was so "off" in my thinking that later on, when I had a chance to plant a church, it was the last thing I wanted to do. During my seminary days, planting a church actually meant you couldn't land a position with a "real" church, so you had to go start one. I didn't want to start a church. I was better than that. The only way I would start a church was in reaction to my disillusionment. If I started a church plant, I wanted to start it pure with a clean slate. (Now, there's a novel thought — as if everything about me is pure as well.) Even if I had to grow into the right motivation, I started Northwood Church, where I now serve, in 1985, and it was an immediate success. Dangerously, deceptively so.

Soon, we had a chance to relocate our church to some property five times our current size. I realize now that the move was way too fast and impetuous. Within a two-month period, we literally came up with the idea, sold our ten acres with our existing building, bought fifty acres, moved to a shopping center, and raised $200,000 to finish it out so we could hold our temporary services in it. I wasn't alone in this risky business—the church voted for it unanimously —except for one of my best friends!

And did we have numbers! The first week we held our service in the shopping center, we grew from 500 in attendance to 700. The numbers continued to astound us. By the end of the month, however, we had "grown" all the way to 350 people. Our church was growing faster in reverse over a three-month period than it had ever grown in drive. As a matter of fact, I had been invited to speak at a program with a well-known church growth author. In the height of our struggle, I offered to bow out of the conference, figuring I would be bad luck. I could see the headlines next to my picture in the brochure: "Ten Ways to Sabotage Your Attendance in Ten Weeks or Less."

During that time, I revisited something Thom Wolf and Carol Davis had said. Thom is the former pastor of Church on Brady that has planted many churches and sent out many missionaries. Carol served on staff with Thom and now heads up her own missions organization. These two individuals began to teach me what I wasn't ready to hear—they began to plant seeds inside of me about what it meant to grow the Church, Capital C, not just my church. Those are two different things altogether. In the following agonizing months, I made a decision. Instead of being the biggest church in the area, we were going to church the area.

Sometimes, what's good for my church isn't always what's good for the Church. And sometimes, frankly, what's good for the Church may actually be bad for my church.

CHURCHING THE AREA

I didn't fully understand the ramifications of that decision at the time. In fact, I'm still discovering and unraveling the mystery of it daily. For example, although I wanted to increase our impact, I didn't know about the process of church multiplication. I was already struggling in the addition department. I knew about church planting, of course, because I was a church planter. However, I didn't realize that healthy churches were *supposed* to be fertile and multiply. Church planting should be as natural as evangelism or discipleship or children's ministry. Despite my lack of understanding exactly what we were doing, we started implementing what it meant to church the area instead of pouring all our energies into becoming the biggest church in the area.

We put the first church plant on the map three miles to the east of us. Soon after, we planted the second church four miles to the west. Today, eight daughter churches encircle our church campus. Suddenly, instead of addition, we were multiplying our numbers exponentially—from 2,000 on our home campus to an additional 5,000 attending church on the eight campuses! Recently, three of those churches had over a thousand for the first time! That has taken ten years. Today, our church has started over eighty churches—that's over 20,000 people who are in church.

Moreover, because every one of our church plants believes in church multiplication, meaning that is part of its DNA, we have many granddaughter, great-granddaughter, and great-great-granddaughter churches—for a total of over 30,000 people in worship every single week. Last year alone, 3,600 new people were in churches that didn't even exist twelve months ago. And most of those churches average 50 to 100 in attendance. Four years from now, they'll all quadruple (at a minimum), making it possible for another 15,000 to 20,000 people to be in church, just from that crop—a single local church.

How did this remarkable growth explosion happen? It did *not* happen because we studied church planting and developed a strategy with systems and goals. I can't sell you a program or a package. It happened because out of my personal brokenness and North-Wood's struggle, we found we could still make a difference. We became frustrated enough to finally realize we were going to have to do some things radically different from what we are doing today if we're going to change the world.

Any missiologist or church historian could have told us that. However, we had to learn it for ourselves firsthand. Ironically, the West faithfully prays for revival and asks the Spirit to do great things in our world today. Let me tell you a secret: Revival has come. It simply hasn't yet come to the West. Revival is happening all over the world in nations like China, which hold valuable secrets for revitalizing the globe.

PUTTING THE CHURCH IN CONTEXT

Why hasn't revival come to the Western church? There are a number of reasons, but I believe the primary reason is that we have taken the church out of context in the West. Instead of allowing it to become what it is meant to be, we have altered it into a more manageable, systematic program that inadvertently dams up the river of God's supernatural work in and among us. Allowing God to transform our perception of the purpose of the church will prompt us to put the church:

- in the context of the nations
- in the context of the culture
- in the context of the kingdom of God
- in the context of the priesthood of the believer
- in the context of eternity

THE CHURCH IN CONTEXT OF THE NATIONS

Imagine the church as a base from which spiritual military operations are designed, planned, formulated, and launched into every corner of the globe and you'll begin to have a picture of a primary theme of Scripture's intent for God's people. "Ask of me, and I will make the nations your inheritance" (Psalm 2:8). Throughout the Old and New Testaments, we see that the nations are important in

God's economy, and discipleship is set within the context of community. Jesus commands us to make disciples of nations, all nations, not merely individuals.

> *A God whose fingerprint is on every ethnos throughout the world loves the nations. This God loves people groups. This God loves governments.*

We are talking about shifting our focus from a reasonable interest in individual personal discipleship to the more daunting corporate task of engaging entire nations and infrastructures. The key word here is *stretch*! We must stretch our thinking beyond ourselves and begin to engage God's heart for the needs of the nations.

A global concept would be difficult to grasp for the band of first-century Jews whose world had only been as large as Galilean shores and greater Palestine. So, Jesus immediately began broadening his disciples' viewpoint of their commission *before* he gave it to them. He had to give them a running start on what he wanted them to do or else they would be overwhelmed. In fact, the Great Commission recorded in Matthew 28 is the climax of the teaching Jesus began much earlier in Matthew 25:31–46:

> When the Son of Man comes in his glory, and all the angels with him, he will sit on his throne in heavenly glory. All the nations will be gathered before him, and he will separate the people one from another as a shepherd separates the sheep from the goats. He will put the sheep on his right and the goats on his left.
>
> Then the King will say to those on his right, "Come, you who are blessed by my Father; take your inheritance, the kingdom prepared for you since the creation of the world. For I was hungry and you gave me something to eat, I was thirsty and you gave me something to drink, I was a stranger and you invited me in, I needed clothes and you clothed me, I was sick and you looked after me, I was in prison and you came to visit me."

Then the righteous will answer him, "Lord, when did we see you hungry and feed you, or thirsty and give you something to drink? When did we see you a stranger and invite you in, or needing clothes and clothe you? When did we see you sick or in prison and go to visit you?"

The King will reply, "I tell you the truth, whatever you did for one of the least of these brothers of mine, you did for me."

Then he will say to those on his left, "Depart from me, you who are cursed, into the eternal fire prepared for the devil and his angels. For I was hungry and you gave me nothing to eat, I was thirsty and you gave me nothing to drink, I was a stranger and you did not invite me in, I needed clothes and you did not clothe me, I was sick and in prison and you did not look after me."

They also will answer, "Lord, when did we see you hungry or thirsty or a stranger or needing clothes or sick or in prison, and did not help you?"

He will reply, "I tell you the truth, whatever you did not do for one of the least of these, you did not do for me."

Then they will go away to eternal punishment, but the righteous to eternal life.

Jesus reveals that at the end of the age, not only is every nation going to be represented before the throne, we are going to be judged as nations. In addition, Scripture outlines the basis of judgment in this passage not on how well we excelled at proclamation but on our practice of feeding the poor and clothing the naked. But what about all the crusades, revivals, street preaching, and mountains of tracts? Where does that fit into Matthew 25?

Having mastered the art of proclamation in the West, we're more comfortable diffusing the strength of the teaching in this passage. We want it to be merely metaphorical. However, Jesus is not presenting an either–or scenario. I believe that the whole of Jesus' teaching is that we will not change the world without the combination of both Billy Graham–type proclamation and Mother Teresa–type service. However, in order for the church to turn the world upside down, it will have to refocus *what* it does in terms of proclamation and service to launch change in the world and, more importantly, *how* it does it.

I began to study God's view of the nations in the Old Testament. What did it look like when God blessed a nation? He impacted their natural infrastructures such as economics, health, education, social services, and so on. How did God accomplish this? Instead of creating a competing infrastructure of religion, he created transformed people who laid across the existing infrastructures through their jobs, home life, and daily traffic patterns. Faith was not an infrastructure in itself, but these transformed people of faith touched every existing infrastructure for the purpose of transforming the culture from the inside out. Today we have turned Christianity into its own infrastructure — competing against the existing culture in largely fruitless efforts. It was never meant to be this way.

THE CHURCH IN CONTEXT OF THE CULTURE

When the early church turned the world upside down, it did so because the church was in the context of the culture — something it hasn't been in the West for a long time. The early church took a strategic stand and emerged from within the culture. It was a natural occurrence: Transformed people living in the culture transformed it relationally. And the process paid off — Christianity spread throughout every province and region. The gospel, divinely planted amidst a lost and dying culture through the very people who carried its message like a virus, infected the culture from within and infiltrated every arena of society.

How did they do it without seminaries, institutions, or at the least a well-designed Sunday school, small groups, or seeker services? These did not yet exist. However, at its onset, the church became a *force from within* the ranks of society to bring about change. When people saw Christianity within the context of community, farmers and workers and maidservants living a transformed life, *their witness* transformed the larger systems and society. Consequently, you will not find evangelistic crusades in the history of the early church. But you will find comprehensive relational evangelism. Programs did not carry the enthusiasm of the gospel in the early church. People did.

> *People have always transmitted the DNA of an effective movement, not programs.*

However, since that time, the church has gradually settled on the side of the culture, bringing pressure to bear *from without* on the culture in a largely fruitless effort to produce change. As Christians, we are too often a force outside of the culture, forcibly trying to push the culture in an opposite direction. Church history is replete with examples of this cyclical strategy. Constantine used government. Luther focused on theology. Revivalism capitalized on evangelistic crusades. Denominationalism wielded methodology. When we bring pressure to bear on the culture to change it in this way, we will never realize lasting results.

Attempts to Change the Culture from the Outside in the Church Used...

Year	Method	Description
312 —	Government	Constantine uses government.
1517 —	Theology	Luther promotes theology.
1792 —	Missions	Carey introduces missions as biography.
1850 —	Revivalism	Revivalism focuses on "the decision."
1890 —	Methodology	Denominations industrialize methodology.

The church is at its best when we are not a force outside the culture but when we are entrenched within the culture. Imagine a set of concentric circles. First, the largest outside circle represents the kingdom. The kingdom of God, in simplest terms, is God's rule and reign over everything. Next, inside of the context of the kingdom is a smaller circle representing the world. The world is fallen and sinful. However, God is at work in the world. How so? Inside of the world, God has established his Church to represent Christ—another smaller circle within the world. Believers are the next smallest inside circle. And inside of each believer is the core—the Holy Spirit (see Figure 1).

In this illustration, we work to bring about change from the inside out. People who are transformed by the Holy Spirit living

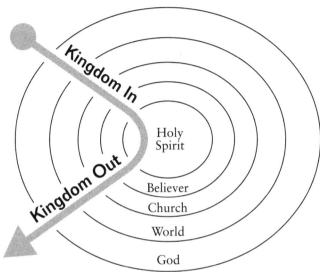

Figure 1

inside of them make their way into the culture of the world and infiltrate it with the undeniable message of a changed life. The kingdom has come into the life of the believer through the indwelling Holy Spirit—Kingdom In. The believer, therefore, goes out into his or her community to engage the world, taking the kingdom with them—Kingdom Out.

In our present-day congregation in Texas, we have a growing number of businesspeople, lawyers, doctors, and the like who are all going into the ministry in our church. The majority of these people have been agnostic or atheists. I can't explain it other than to say people are moving to our bedroom community and technology-based area, and God is capturing their hearts. They are being transformed to such a degree that they want to leave their jobs and their vocations to start churches. In fact, one of my biggest problems is trying to keep doctors in the medical field and lawyers in the legal fields instead of leaving their training all behind for the mission field. We encourage them to use their jobs, not leave their jobs, because their job is their venue into the very mission field they love. This is the living example of the early church.

I constantly remind our people that they have more of a platform to witness and change the culture submerged in the culture than they do outside the culture.

THE CHURCH IN THE CONTEXT OF THE KINGDOM OF GOD

We must recognize that we've taken the church out of the context of the nations and the context of the culture, but we've also taken it out of the related context of the kingdom. If God loves the nations, and he does, we have to do more than love what we see in our own backyards if we're going to plug into the kingdom. When we're more concerned about our own fiefdom than God's kingdom, we will believe being the biggest church is more important than churching the communities around us. We may challenge our laypeople with dreams of becoming the largest church in the area (and God is not opposed to church growth), but many believers dream of more than brick and mortar.

I learned early on in my experience when we moved our church to the shopping center, if we strive to be the church for the area, we do things one way. However, when we strive to be a church for the kingdom—for the communities and ultimately for the nations—we expand our strategy beyond ourselves. We don't plant churches for communities. We plant them for the world, basing them in local communities. Simply said, we don't have anything big enough to challenge the church when we limit ourselves to what we can see with our confined vision.

Let me clarify that this isn't about producing more missionaries from our congregations (though God is not opposed to calling out more missionaries); rather, we're talking about something bigger than that. We begin to develop a kingdom mindset by dreaming out the fullest extent of the answer to the question, *What if the church were the missionary?* Blue sky it. Picture the whole church body, functioning as the missionary in the world today. *That's* putting the church in the context of the kingdom.

When we understand that God doesn't call people to preach as much as he calls preachers and other people to the kingdom, we have the church in the right context. When we understand equipping people for kingdom work is very different from merely making converts, we have the church in the right context. Converts may grow the church, but the caliber of disciples required to change the world and operate in the larger realm of the kingdom is much, much different.

I believe the Great Commission was and is given to the church, not just individuals. And certainly not solely to the "special" people we've designated as vocational missionaries. As a missionary to India, William Carey did in the late eighteenth century what we need to do today. He restored the call to vocational missionaries; however, we must believe God wants to expand and restore that call within the church as a whole. In 1792, missions focused on biography; in the 1900s missions became institutions and organizations. In the twenty-first century, missions translates to kingdom—it's everyone, everywhere, and every infrastructure. Not just religious vocational workers, but everyone!

Is the church the only true vessel for the kingdom of God? No, but it is the local, practical expression of it—and the most underutilized vehicle for expanding the kingdom at that. Instead of attempting to change society by more religious vocational workers, we ought to focus on utilizing people who are already on the "inside" secular markets who are sitting in our pews.

THE CHURCH IN THE CONTEXT OF THE WHOLE WORLD

" . . . and you will be my witnesses in Jerusalem, and in all Judea and Samaria, and to the ends of the earth" (Acts 1:8).

Contrary to many institutions' ideologies (and most charts and graphs in the backs of Bibles), when Jesus gave the Great Commission, he was not implying that it was sequential—as in step 1, step 2, step 3. It was not to Jerusalem, then on to Judea, then to Samaria, and finally to the ends of the earth. It was—and is—both/and. It's one *and* two *and* three *and* four. *One and two and three and four.*

What we have mistaken for something of a sequence is really more like a song. The tempo requires every beat, without rests. One stanza leading into another and forming the melody. It means doing all we can as a local church to reach the whole world simultaneously, while at the same time recognizing that one style alone will not reach them. Out of that conviction, we begin to start other churches to reach other segments of the world. We begin operating within our communities, statewide, nationally, and ultimately adopting an Unreached People Group (UPG) internationally as well. At no other time in the history of communication and technology has it been as feasible for the church to operate in all dimensions simultaneously. So, why aren't we doing so?

East and West Have Met

Unfortunately, for most churches, missions is not the song it is meant to be but a coda—which in Italian literally means "the tail." In that sense, missions is an add-on in the church system that takes place once a year (preferably in the fall in the fellowship hall) and involves booth after booth of pictures of people so remotely connected to our daily existence and treated as distant and unrelated. They are the people "over there."

In reality, East and West have met. They are merging in every modern arena except the church.

Mother Teresa has said of herself, "By blood and origin I am Albanian. My citizenship is Indian. I am a Catholic nun. As to my calling, I belong to the whole world. As to my heart, I belong entirely to the heart of Jesus."[1] Doing church in the context of the whole world changes everything. Missions become core to who we are, not something we do as an add-on. (Incidentally, I don't like the word *missions*. It's not even biblical. It's a tradition we formulated on our own when we should be more *missional* in our thinking.)

Remember, the kingdom is inside of transformed believers with salty lives who can't help but have the light of Jesus flow out of them all the time. It's a natural consequence. Churches *will* be planted, people *will* become disciples, congregations *will* grow, if only we'll get it in the right context. We will know *what* to do and *why* we're doing it when we put the church in the context of a whole-world church plant movement. When we begin to see the role of a foreign diplomat as tantamount to a professional missionary, we're on our way to understanding what it means to be a world citizen who goes way beyond Western philosophy in search of impact.

A World Citizen

When my son applied to New York University, he defined what it means to be a world citizen in practical terms.

> I've grown up in a pastor's home, but not a typical pastor's home. Dad started our church to help people and the world. It has meant building schools, orphanages, clinics, and conducting business in developing nations. As a result, I have grown up in a home with foreign dignitaries, educators, doctors, and businesspeople and a view of life that says, "As global citizens, we must make the world a better place." Buddhist, Communist, Muslims, Middle Easterners, Far Easterners, Near Easterners, African, Athiest, Hindus, Agnostics, Jews and yes, even Christians are all a part of my network. It sounds confusing, but it works.

As global citizens, we begin to see ourselves in a new network that trumps the anemic idea of "mission-mindedness" in exchange for being missional and kingdom focused.

THE CHURCH IN THE CONTEXT OF THE PRIESTHOOD OF THE BELIEVER

Theologically, the traditional meaning behind the phrase "the priesthood of the believer" has meant open access to the throne of God. The Father can speak to each believer without depending on another person to mediate for us (Hebrews 7–10). In the context of becoming a world citizen, it means recognizing doctors, administrators, executives, and secretaries as equally valid and available means of transferring the gospel to the nations. Everyone has an innate sense that we ought to be making a difference and an equally innate sense to know when we're not.

The context of the priesthood of the believer unleashes a radically new missionary force unlike the world has seen since the first-century church. It's no longer about missionaries using platforms; it's believers sharing their trade and their faith. Some people who teach the doctrine of the priesthood of the believer use it primarily as the right to my own interpretation and hearing—but it is far more than that. It is the ability to hear God specifically call me and use me to make a difference in the world, just like anyone else.

I Want to Become a Christian and You Won't Let Me

Recently, our church helped lead a young Hindu man who was attending our church to meet the Lord. I first met Pukar when he was a waiter at a restaurant where I was eating. I did the pastoral thing and invited him to church, but I really didn't expect to see him. I couldn't believe it when he showed up one Sunday! It was perhaps the first time he'd been in a church, so it was fascinating to observe his reaction. We invited him to Sunday lunch with my family, so he rode with my son to the restaurant. On the way over, he announced to Ben in his thick accent, "I think I want to be a Christian. I am a Hindu, but in America I will worship Jesus." My son has traveled the world with me, but this one was a hard one, so he told Pukar, "You need to talk to my dad."

After we ate together, I inquired about Pukar's interest in church and faith. Pukar seized the moment and told me Jesus was a "good God for America" and he respected Jesus. I went on to explain to him that there was only one God, and his name is Jesus. We just cannot add Jesus to a shelf of gods. Without hesitation, he smiled and told me, "I can."

I knew I wasn't going to convince this young man of monotheism in one sitting. So we worked at becoming good friends. We lifted weights together, and we welcomed Pukar in our home a number of times. I had been to Nepal, so he saw my pictures and we visited about his home country whenever he became homesick or lonely. Soon, others in the church grew to know and love Pukar just as my family had.

One Sunday, God directed me during a time of worship to lead the church in prayer instead of preaching my sermon. With many at the altar praying, I sensed someone kneel right beside me. His body was heaving, he was weeping so intensely. It was Pukar. I prayed with him, that God would reveal himself one day to Pukar and use him to one day bring great hope to his people. Pukar is a member of a significant family, studying here in the States. That put him in a peculiar position that I dare say none of us has ever considered. In order for him to renounce all other gods and worship God alone, he would have to concede that he himself was not a god!

Pukar went back to his seat and the service concluded soon after. As usual, lots of people were milling about in the lobby after the service. Pukar found me in the crowd, looked me straight in the eye, and announced before everyone, "I want to become a Christian and you won't let me!" Now that's something pastors don't hear every day.

I told him, "I will Pukar, but you have to mean it and you have to believe there is only one God. I don't want you to do this just because you love us and want to be our friends — we will be your friend regardless. Committing to Christ could be a high price for you in your position. I want you to know what you're getting into."

He replied, "I am a grown man, Bob. I can decide for myself. I want to be a Christian. I believe there is only one God, Jesus."

What else could I say? He invited Christ into his life that day, and God began to use him in powerful ways. He soon led another friend to Christ, an agnostic American who happened to be one of the most popular rave DJs in the metroplex. Standing in the baptistery one day weeks later with a former Hindu and an agnostic, now brothers in Christ, reminded me in a dramatic fashion that the potential for globalization is in the church today, and the individual believer is key.

A New Kind of Missionary

What if God really has called the church as the missionary? (Wait a minute. That's not strategic enough! It can't be programmed!) Not necessarily, but that's what it looks like to put the church back in its proper contexts—in the context of entire nations, in the context of the culture, and in the context of the kingdom. For the church to be leveled on top of the culture and across infrastructures, early church style, we must equip the church to be the missionary. The laypeople in the early church carried the gospel as they traveled the transportation routes so that it would take root in individual cities. Today's information exchange and business climate offer a similar convergence with the early church experience where the people who work at IBM, Mobil, and in the health professions have unprecedented access to lost people throughout the world. In fact, a mobilized laity is the only way—not a nice or creative or appeasing way, but the only way the world will hear about Jesus.

Entrepreneurial leaders will not wait for sluggish churches to engage the world. They are already doing it from home through their computers every day! Sadly, the church is not initiating this movement. Rather, international business, travel, and communications are the prompters for people to get in touch with one another and begin to forge relationships around the globe. However, even if we didn't start the conversation with the world, it's not too late to join in. If the church waits to get in on the global conversation with the message of the gospel, we threaten the contribution these current legions of workers (many of whom are already believers) could make to the expansion of the kingdom.

As the developing world becomes more effective in reaching their own cultures and educated in their ability to share their stories, the role of the Westerner will continue to diminish—unless we equip and promote the nationals for key positions of leadership. The practice of paternalistic missions is over (even as it continues to serve as an anemic model in some places). Kingdom extension expands exponentially when nationals are the ones doing the work, not the ones solely on the receiving end of service. I'm intrigued by think tanks and conferences I attend where a roomful of Caucasians discuss our need to engage the world.

However, if God is placing avant-garde soldiers like Pukar throughout infrastructures that cross nations and ethnicities in order to be present in every culture, the church is going to have to recognize this well-suited new breed of "missionaries" and get on with it!

THE CHURCH IN THE CONTEXT OF ETERNITY

Kevin Kelly is one of the researchers for the Long Now Project[2]—a giant 10,000-year clock that many other scientists and sociologists are building (think Stonehenge). A prototype is currently on display in the Science Museum in London, England. Powered by seasonal temperatures, it ticks once a year, bongs once a century, and cuckoos every millennium. (To give some perspective, it has been a millennium since the last ice age. No one remembers it.) The motive behind the Clock of the Long Now is to treat the last 10,000 years as last week and the next 10,000 years as next week in order to emphasize the partnership between time and responsibility. If we believe our present generation may be the last generation of humankind, we will selfishly use up every resource for our own existence and hence rob from the future.

Church of the Long Now

What does a curious clock have to do with the church today? Not much, unless we recall that what we are doing today in the church will affect the church tomorrow. What if we became the Church of the Long Now, realizing we only have now to act but also recognizing that *how we act* creates futures (both positive and negative) down the line that we can't even envision today? In other words, putting the church back into the context of eternity requires that we have to learn to slow down and think deliberately about what we are doing so we can build for future generations. Elise Bouding, a sociologist, is quoted as saying, "If one is mentally out of breath all the time from dealing with the present, there is no energy left for imagining the future."[3]

As evangelicals, we are familiar with a historical precedence of an eternal view of life, but at the same time we've convinced ourselves we only have a short time to accomplish all we wish to do. We are too often the Church of the Panicked Rush and Hurry It Up because of the tyranny of the urgent instead of the Church of the Long Now.

The result of rushing toward eternity is often shortsighted responsibility of the gospel and a hurried perspective on what God calls us to do.

Fear or Faith?

Faith is a long-term perspective toward others realizing a future reward. In contrast, fear is a short term, me-centered "now" that gets it all now, but nothing for the future. We may win hundreds to the Lord in one night, but the test will be the daily discipleship of those new believers. What happens fast is illusion; what happens slowly is reality. The job of the long view is to penetrate illusion. Edward Gibbons wrote, "The more gradual and hidden the change, the more important it turned out to be."[4] Rosabeth Moss Kanter wrote, "Bad things happen fast—war, fire, earthquakes; good things happen slow—society."[5]

We don't often think deeply and act responsibly with our faith on the whole, but what would it look like if we did? If we took an eternal perspective to infiltrate the whole culture everywhere, we would have plenty of time to do what God has called us to do. We wouldn't all be strategists, but we would all keep our feet moving. If we understood time in this context, our response to the future and how we establish the kingdom would be dramatically altered. Our only hope of significant development of the nations and engaging the world will be more long-term views of our impact that understand the church in all its proper contexts.

QUESTIONS TO THINK ABOUT AND TALK ABOUT

1. What do you see as the difference between "doing missions" and "living the kingdom of God"?

2. How would your life be different if you viewed your vocation as your primary ministry?

3. What practical difference is your church making in your community beyond worship services?

4. If we believed Jesus would not return for another two thousand years, how would our life and ministry be different?

Three

WHY ARE WE GROWING CHURCHES APART FROM TRANSFORMATION?

Our church is in a primarily white suburban community. Recently, we baptized a family of Pakistani Muslims, a family of east African Muslims, a Vietnamese Buddhist, a Korean Buddhist, and three or four backslidden Baptists—all in one month. Several weeks after the Vietnamese Buddhist accepted Christ, "John" boarded a plane to Afghanistan because his job transferred him there during the war with Afghanistan to run the restaurant for the military air base. Do you think it's any accident that the whole spiritual course of John's life changed before receiving this reassignment? I believe he got reassigned in more ways than one. He was reassigned into the kingdom of God spiritually when he accepted Christ, and then he was reassigned from a restaurant manager to a twenty-first-century missionary on foreign soil.

We had an informal commissioning service of sorts for him after his baptism, during which he aired the irony saying, "I'm a Buddhist trying to be a Christian. How am I going to witness to a Muslim?"

What could I tell him to do? I simply said in response, "Just tell them what Jesus did for you. Live it out. That's all you can do."

John's life was radically, irreversibly changed. His story is ringing true throughout Afghanistan today.

Another young man in our church grew up with an agnostic father. "Paul" became an agnostic like his dad, even though his mom eventually became a Christian and brought him to our church half the time. When Paul reached adulthood, he decided to join the Marines—who promptly shipped him off to boot camp in Southern California. A few weeks later, he emailed me the news that he had found Christ and wanted to be baptized in our church. I'm still not entirely sure how boot camp brought him to Christ, but it did. So he flew back one weekend for us to baptize him.

That Sunday I preached on the role the Roman soldiers played in the spread of the gospel throughout the ends of the earth—just as Paul would soon have the opportunity to do. He publicly announced his commitment to Christ through the picture of baptism and we commissioned him as a missionary to Iraq in the same day. I remember telling him, "You're under orders by our president, but don't you ever forget you're first under orders by the King of kings." God transformed a young man's life in the Marines to serve his country and to spread the news of Jesus Christ overseas.

EVANGELISM OVERHAUL

Because of these stories and countless others, I'm convinced the greatest hope we have of seeing our culture transformed is first *to make the gospel clear in our practice of evangelism.* My church is a very contemporary church. We're an innovative church. Some would say we're off the wall, but I refuse to compromise about what it means to accept Christ. I'm not into feel-good theology, giving people bits and pieces of Scripture to make their lives a little bit better. I want people to get the whole load so that they understand the gospel ultimately changes our eternal destinies and is supposed to infinitely change us here and now. We must be transformed.

In my tribe, we're known for morality (at least our views on morality). But we're not necessarily known for being transformed people. Raised in East Texas in the home of a Baptist pastor, we never smoked or drank. Our elders told us, "Never chew—or run around with girls who do." But someone could be incredibly mean, and that was just being a good Baptist.

How can that be? Our understanding of personal transformation is inextricably tied to our understanding of evangelism. Misunderstand evangelism, and we'll misunderstand the end results of our effort. The church is artful and extremely skillful in our practice of Christianity today, but I do not believe that we understand evangelism. We don't have a grasp on the fact that the whole concept starts with the heart.

How Did They Do It?

How did the early church grow so incredibly fast? They didn't have an educated clergy; they didn't have the money; they didn't have the buildings. They didn't have anything that we do. They didn't even have the printed Bible to argue over. Given the fact that most of them couldn't read or write, how could they do it so fast?

Most of them were oral learners. What they heard, they believed. And what they believed transformed them so radically that people in their midst said, "This stuff is real," and other people wanted it. That's the winning strategy. It wasn't because a group of preachers came up with a promising plan. It was because of preachers who led laypeople to live it day in and day out, and the result was that it transformed everything.

The poor and uneducated masses have followed Christianity by this very means for centuries up until the present. They could not understand systematic theology or modern ministry management techniques, but they understand better than most injustice and suffering. Jesus appealed to the masses because he was someone who identified with them, who lived with them and was like them—a homeless God. They could accept that kind of God. No longer doomed to a caste below others and not trusting in good works and martyrdom, his mercy drew and continues to draw the masses to him.

Today, however, even the poor in Third World countries are becoming more educated. More young people are born every day with access to knowledge and information. Already in most major cities of the world, even the youngest poor have general knowledge that the king's advisors did not have access to 150 years ago! And they are asking questions before they are responding in mass to the gospel—questions and issues that the church has too long ignored or streamlined in order not to have to deal with them. The day when the church could get away with that is passing. We cannot ignore tough questions in order to fast track people onto our church membership rolls. We cannot circumvent contradictions in our push for conversion.

"How do we know there is a God?"

In order to carry on a conversation about God in non-Christian global cultures, one must always start with the existence of God, the nature of revelation of his Word, the Bible, and Jesus. Never start with the "Roman Road," an evangelistic tract, or merely extending verses on how to become a Christian. Most of those approaches are based on a familiar knowledge or acquaintance with the message. That is no longer the case.

> As a result of the information explosion, philosophical—not historical—apologetics will become our mainstay of evangelism if we are going to transform the world locally and globally.

Frequently on Sunday mornings at our church I'll address the issue of the existence of God with questions like, "How do we know there is a God?" I give the people the basic and simple steps to grow in their understanding of creation and the like, but all good theology and explanation is just that—basic and simple. We must never forget Jesus gave the gospel to the masses, not preachers, pastors, and theologians. We have to explain it in language the common person can understand.

The point is that I want people to know more than just, "I know there is a God because I feel him in my heart." That won't go far in most of the world today. I'm convinced we must be very clear in our presentation of the gospel and the rationale for God's existence. However, I'm also convinced we have to reconsider how people *respond* to our evangelistic efforts.

Closing the Door on Conversion

In the past, my typical response to evangelism has been to open the door and let everybody in. Now, I think we need to close it. Revivalist preachers like Jonathan Edwards, Gilbert Tennant, or John Wesley wouldn't know what to make of the modern-day church invitation. It would baffle them to see that somebody could walk into church out of the clear blue, hear a sermon, come down the aisle, and pray a prayer. Boom — conversion. They have the whole deal in thirty seconds.

You see, conversion as we tout it today misses something. To Wesley or Whitefield or Edwards, it was not just a matter of praying the prayer. It was not, as Willard would say, "the gospel of self-improvement." Theirs was a message of sweeping transformation. Today we would have baptized Jonathan Edwards when he was thirteen, and we would have baptized a lost man if you know the history of his life. It wasn't until he was in his early twenties that he really found God. He was not merely converted at that time; he was transformed. Conversion has lost its meaning. You can convert — change religions — but stay the same person on the whole.

Decisions That Matter

As we come out of the industrial age, part of our challenge in communicating the gospel to the rest of the world will be allowing people to process. The journals of John Wesley, Charles Spurgeon, and others remind us that they never rushed people as many try to do today. People would struggle and pray, and sometimes it would go on for days, but when they made a decision it mattered, and it lasted. We must instill the truth that evangelism is not just an event where someone prays the sinner's prayer. It is a process of awakening and understanding that comes only through the Holy Spirit.

When that process is short-circuited, rushed, or streamlined for the sake of church industry and production, we often get the stat but lose the soul.

Our best converts at NorthWood have been our agnostics and atheists.

Am I Different?

Because I travel around the world and speak frequently to young pastors and college students, I'm often asked from Christians and non-Christians alike what I think about different religions. Christian bookstores are filled with great books detailing the differences. However, the real issue in evangelism and in the world today is not, "How is Christianity different?" but "How has Christianity made me different?"

We have exchange students from around the world in our church every week. We often encourage our members to open their homes for a year to allow a Muslim, a Buddhist, a Hindu, an animist, or an atheist to come and live with them. It's one way they will see that being a Christian is more than being a nice person. They'll hopefully see the ins and outs of a believer's faith and how it makes a difference in daily life. It makes for exciting and unpredictable episodes in youth Sunday school!

At times, some parents have been upset when these kids would introduce their ideas in class—but what a wonderful opportunity the church has to engage young people in diverse conversations. Think how much better it is to have your child learn to deal with these issues in youth group rather than to leave home and have to deal with them apart from the church setting. We fear exposing our children to different ideas and people. Often the church today is monastic in its approach. That just won't work for the future.

Buddhas at the Preacher's Home

I was out of town on an extended international lecture trip when our own international student arrived to stay with us for a year. My wife, Nikki, and our children, Ben and Jill, were there to welcome Ti as he arrived at the airport and drive him to our home. As are most internationals, he was an extremely polite and conscientious young man. His family was excited when they heard he would be living with a "minister." In their culture, that meant a government official. When they found out it was instead a "pastor," they started watching the television show *Seventh Heaven* to find out what it was like in a pastor's home. (Was he in for a surprise!)

Upon his arrival, Ti and his family wanted to honor us with a gift. He carried with him a carefully wrapped gift that he had purchased in his homeland. When Nikki arrived home, he proudly presented my wife with the gift—four small, carved buddhas, one for each member of my family. Careful not to hurt his feelings, Nikki thanked him for his thoughtfulness.

"Bob," she said when she called me later that night to tell me what had happened, "I wasn't sure what to do with them, so I left them on the stairs for you." Now, that was a dilemma—a Christian pastor with foreign gods on display in his home. Though I travel the globe, I never buy other "gods." Gradually, the four buddhas made their way into more "obscure" places—enough said!

It is easy for us to understand how a Hindu must forsake his gods and believe in only one God in order to become a Christian. But though Americans in general would claim to be monotheists (if they believe in God at all), the reality is most of us have many gods. They just aren't a group or clan like Shiva and his gods. When we are ready to dethrone our gods and give complete control to Jesus, then we can ask him to forgive us of our sins and sin nature and to come into our life. We make a decision to repent of our sins and make him the Lord of our life. That's conversion.

We worship one God, and that makes all the difference in who we are. What makes us so different, or should make us so different? And if we are not different, what does that say?

Change from the Inside Out

Most religious people are good—good-natured, good-hearted individuals. But despite their outward sincerity, inside they live apart from the truth. If Christ is the truth and he lives in us, shouldn't there be something qualitatively different about us other than a goodness quotient? Now, if I were being a good pastor, I would have started with our guest's foreign gods. I would have insisted he put those away and maybe given him some tracts on truth and error. You see, when we realize that change is what someone needs, we often tackle it as church leaders and even individuals from the outside in. We are good at identifying behaviors to change or specific information to be learned. We force it externally in the hopes that it will mystically reach internally.

But if you examine the quality of disciples the church is producing today, you will see it doesn't work that way. Why? It is the opposite of how God works. He works from the inside out. The only way we will ever really be different is if something has taken place internally first. If a church is going to be an effective church, one of the most obvious characteristics will have to be the kind of people that it turns out. Jesus taught that the kingdom is first internal then external. Jesus said in Luke 17:21 that the kingdom of God is within you. That is just unfathomable. How can God live inside of us and not make a difference? He cannot; he *will* make a difference, or we must question whether he lives inside of us at all.

Moving from Conversion to Transformation—the Myths

I've come to dislike the word *conversion*. It no longer communicates as it used to communicate. Today, to "convert" means to change religion, from one religion to another. It's more of a belief system than an actual lifestyle. When explaining the impact Christianity should have on us, I prefer the word *transformation*. Unless we are altogether transformed into the image of Christ in how we live and behave, we are no different from any other religion in the world promising enlightenment and self-improvement.

The only way we will ever be different will be because we have moved from conversion to transformation.

We are talking about a completely different way of life and living. What does it look like? Jesus described it in the Sermon on the Mount. Hold on though—it is not something that is easily lived (definitely not with our old ways of learning).

> Therefore, I urge you, brothers, in view of God's mercy, to offer your bodies as living sacrifices, holy and pleasing to God—this is your spiritual act of worship. Do not conform any longer to the pattern of this world, but be transformed by the renewing of your mind. Then you will be able to test and approve what God's will is—his good, pleasing and perfect will.
>
> For by the grace given me I say to every one of you: Do not think of yourself more highly than you ought, but rather think of yourself with sober judgment, in accordance with the measure of faith God has given you. (Romans 12:1 – 3)

The journey of transformation begins with legitimate conversion. To convert means to change over, to switch. Following are some myths about conversion that make it difficult for us to understand what it actually entails.

First, there is a myth that *conversion means making a better me*, improving who I am. However, Scripture contradicts that theory because it teaches we are totally lost and depraved apart from God. Conversion is far more than taking a lost person and conquering bad habits.

There is also the myth that *conversion means praying the "sinner's prayer."* This is wrong; it's more than mouthing words. It's possible to pray the sinner's prayer and not be converted. First John 2:3 says, "We know that we have come to know him" because we obey his commands. We know it by the kind of life we are producing.

You may be familiar with a lingering myth that *conversion is the epitome of spirituality*. No, it's just the beginning. Churches who gauge themselves by baptisms, attendance, and membership do not emphasize what we are producing as much as how fast we are producing it. The numbers of conversions are reflected in denominational reports and are the thrust of building programs, but still bankrupt churches have littered the land over the past twenty years. We know conversion is not the end all of spirituality. What numbers do you talk about the most?

Many churches inadvertently promote the myth that *conversion means going to church and jumping through hoops.* Sometimes the hoops we maneuver in our attempt to be more religious take us further from God, not closer. Sunday school pins and certificates, confirmation classes—all these can be good, but when the process is the focus instead of the relationship, they lose their power. We may wind up with smarter, more well-informed converts that do all we ask them to, but does it transform them?

I have a good friend who is a Japanese American from a charismatic background. I'm from a Baptist background, although neither of us would claim total allegiance to our camps anymore! He once jokingly said to me about churches and giving, "You Baptists use guilt in your offerings to get money. We Charismatics use greed! Greed will always get more than guilt!" He's right! We all know people should give out of love and obedience, but when that fails, we resort to other things we think will help. However, those tactics often ultimately undermine what we're trying to do.

Of course, some buy into the myth that *conversion is nice but not total,* allowing one to continue to have a secular and spiritual dichotomy. However, Jesus taught that there is no separation in the life of the believer of the secular and spiritual; we are one being. We used to understand that; tragically, many don't anymore. The Muslims are attracting attention in today's society because they don't separate the two, and yet our society tolerates that. Islamic spirituality is their everyday reality and it drives everything that they do politically and practically. We fear this philosophy in the West. Because of the worldliness of some believers, perhaps we *should* fear it; they've adopted the political strategies and work of the world to achieve their ends.

Finally, there is the myth that *conversion is primarily fire insurance*. Wrong! That's only a benefit and not the motivation.

A NEW APPROACH TO DISCIPLESHIP

In today's world, not only should we rethink our presentation of the gospel and a person's response to evangelism, but we should design a completely new approach to discipleship. Evangelism and discipleship (the process of transformation) go hand in hand. The "love of Christ" compels us toward transformation—a relationship motivates us toward change. That is the heartbeat of discipleship that the information-based emphasis has muffled. The challenge must be first to redefine evangelism—that it's people's hearts we're after, not their behavior. And then we must redefine what discipleship is all about.

It's Not What You Know That Counts

I'm not sure that our old definition of discipleship served us well in the past when things were stable and uniform. However, there is no doubt that without a new form of discipleship and a new understanding of what that means and how it is worked out, we will not survive the future. The quality of what we are producing in the West not only produces "defeated" and "depressed" Christians, but it has little or no hope of changing the community where the church is located, let alone a bigger world. To engage local communities and global spheres will require a radically different kind of disciple than what we have produced so far.

The only way we will ever be different is if the practice of Christianity is more important than the instruction. The gauge is not how much a person knows but how that person lives. From worship, to group life, to children and youth ministry, most churches focus primarily on instruction. Most discipleship emphasis in churches centers on books, Scripture memory, and Bible studies that are information-based. No one would dare contend that we are changing our culture and world because of that single-handed effort. In fact, the unintended result is that a participant can graduate from level to level, learning more information without changing from the inside out.

I long to be more than I am. Don't you? But isn't it frustrating to run after our favorite Bible teachers and jump from one new Bible study or new teaching like ping-pong balls looking for a person with a secret to lasting personal change? Many run after favorite fads because they haven't stopped long enough to look at the favorite Son. Christianity is about radical change—but we just can't seem to pull it off. Why? Because we have not crossed over from being merely a convert to being a disciple. The biggest challenge today is producing a different kind of disciple.

> *Converts grow a church, but disciples change the world.*

From Information to Transformation

The emphasis in discipleship must shift from information to transformation. Information downloading is easy. In contrast, transformational living doesn't require huge amounts of information, but it does require the consistent practice of what you know. Most Christians believe enough already, but their practice is woefully low. How is it that we can believe the right things and yet it does not make a difference in our life? Because we've lost sight of how God works to promote right living.

Right living doesn't come from more information but from more imitation. Instruction and practice must be merged. One practical thing we have tried to do at our church is to merge it through synchronizing what we talk about in worship with our focus in small groups and with our members' personal worship. For example, we focus on the Sermon on the Mount in a consistent manner from a corporate to a relational to a personal level.

Deep Moments of Learning

Whenever we apply the truth, it prevents overfamiliarity because we are not merely informed but empowered. Application of what we know in our heads creates the deep moments of learning in all of us. At that point, we refuse to let materialism, pragmatism, or self-centeredness control us—something that only the Holy Spirit can accomplish. John 14–16 teaches us that the Spirit convicts us, guides us, comforts us, and empowers us. He is at the front end of conversion and thoroughly involved thereafter. "He saved us, not because of righteous things we had done, but because of his mercy. He saved us through the washing of rebirth and renewal by the Holy Spirit" (Titus 3:5).

The Holy Spirit is not optional to those who would be transformed. In fact, true spiritual transformation is impossible apart from him—especially in today's culture. How else can we love our enemies, bless those who curse us, turn the other cheek, or give away our possessions to the poor? In short, how can we act like Jesus apart from the Spirit of Jesus? We cannot. Oh, we can try for a while, but it's just too difficult. He is required; there simply is no other way.

In Matthew 16:16–19, Simon Peter said to Jesus, "You are the Christ, the Son of the living God." Jesus replied, "Blessed are you, Simon son of Jonah, for this was not revealed to you by man, but by my Father in heaven. And I tell you that you are Peter, and on this rock I will build my church, and the gates of Hades will not overcome it. I will give you the keys of the Kingdom of heaven; whatever you bind on earth will be bound in heaven, and whatever you loose on earth will be loosed in heaven." This is utterly incredible! We have been given the keys to the kingdom, yet we struggle to be effective Christians at the most basic level.

What Do We Want from Jesus?

In reality, if we are content with conversion instead of transformation, it is because we don't want that much from Jesus. We want salvation and some peppy information to make us happy, but when it comes to integrating our inmost being with what Christ said he would do with us, we don't want that. It can be too costly. Knowing Christ and following him is far more than what Dallas Willard has insightfully termed, "sin management." Most of us want that out of God, but there is so much more!

I once heard Peter Drucker address several hundred pastors in Denver. In his initial remarks he said he wanted us to know that he couldn't claim to be a Christian, only hope to be. He explained that the title "Christian" was given to the early believers by unbelievers because their behavior was said to be so much like Christ. He said that for him to call himself a Christian is one thing, but "for others to recognize it in me" is quite another. It was powerful. For him, Christianity was far more than a religion; it was a lifestyle. Teasingly, as I passed him in the hall I asked him, "So, Mr. Drucker, would you like to become a Christian? I will help you!" He once again restated his position — a powerful one that emulates the focus of real transformation. The question now is, how do we produce that kind of disciple?

QUESTIONS TO THINK ABOUT AND TALK ABOUT

1. Why does believing the right things not necessarily lead to right behaviors?
2. How is conversion different from transformation?
3. How is the gospel making me different right now in my life?
4. If I were living in the early church, would lost people readily call me a Christian? Why or why not?

Part Two

T-LIFE:

Creating a Culture for Personal Transformation

Because many of today's Christians have become so enmeshed with the world, we have determined we can stay as we are, keep all we have, give some, and do some good. When it comes down to it, many people are looking for a little spiritual spit shine and self-help, not transformation. However, for God to use us to turn the world upside down as he intends, internal transformation must happen. Out of our church has emerged a model called "Transformed Life," which we abbreviate to "T-Life." Our mind, our emotions, our very being, the very nature of our heart must not be improved but transformed. This is why we call it l-i-f-e. That transformation takes place by living out the truths of the teachings of Jesus.

The center of T-Life is the desire to glorify God amid a radically different approach to discipleship. This combines an early church

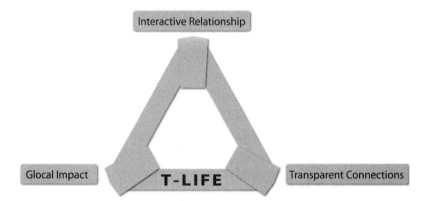

model of discipleship with an emerging Eastern church model. The Western approach to discipleship is the transfer of information through fill-in-the-blank-format curricula. It assumes information will impact beliefs and, therefore, behavior. In contrast, T-Life focuses on creating a culture, not a curriculum. This culture fosters a kind of transformation gauged more by lifestyle and impact on the family, the community, and the world than by graduating to the next Bible class. The premise is simple. The former quest for information made us smarter, but not more holy or transformed or any more connected with the culture or world in terms of impact. T-Life envisions something greater.

The T-Life model has three core elements:

Interactive relationship with God: the combination of God, a Bible, pen, journal, soft music, and Starbucks in order for great things to happen

Transparent connections: people who are learning to interact with God making authentic connections with other believers

Glocal impact: convergence of life, ministry, and vocation — the bridge between a person's vocation and ministry that spans community development locally and globally

Four

WHEN WILL JESUS BE ENOUGH?

Interactive relationship with God
the combination of God, a Bible, pen, journal, soft music,
and Starbucks in order for great things to happen

A couple of years ago, we decided that we would write a curriculum on how to put T-Life together and on what we were learning about how spiritual transformation takes place—a foolish step back to the old mindset that assumes information changes behavior! (See how insidious it is?) My motivation was pure. I wanted to know more about how I could raise up more men and women using their jobs to engage the world and to help mobilize more missionaries moving all over the world.

Thus, we handpicked twenty successful Christians in our church for a think tank, most of whom had been agnostic or atheists but were now spiritually transformed and making an impact in the world. When I told them my idea, they shot it down before it was even out of the gate. They all agreed in unison, "Bob, this isn't a curriculum. It's a culture that's been created at NorthWood." So we began to study the culture of NorthWood and see what we could learn. We began to ask, "What was it about the culture of North-Wood that made it so unique?"

INTERACTIVE RELATIONSHIP WITH GOD

The beginning of the whole T-Life disciple begins with an interactive relationship with God. We're talking about a free-flowing relationship with God. We typically don't even use the word "worship" because it means so many different things to different people. This interactive spiritual discipline requires that we read God's Word and respond to it. God isn't just someone we believe in, it's someone with whom we commune.

Reading the Bible

What we began to do in our church in the early days was to push people to read through the Bible every year—primarily to educate them to God's Word. Remember, many of our people were new Christians. We didn't understand at the time the significance of what we were doing until we began to see the results. When we started practicing our interactive relationship with God, we began to grasp a deeper understanding of the living nature of the Word of God. People began to experience the fact that the Bible is a living book. When they got up early in the morning with their Bible and journal, they were quiet enough to hear God impress his truth on them out of his Word.

Listening Skills Are Important

Another thing we didn't understand at the time or realize we were doing is that we were also teaching our people listening skills. Hearing God has become an art with specialized books that teach us to "read the wind" when we're in a crisis or have a major decision to make. In contrast, in the early church hearing God and knowing his will was a basic life discipline, not a crisis situation. We learn to see him and recognize him in every event throughout the day when we start on our knees and his Word. But it's *how* we read it that makes all the difference.

We teach our people to begin their day with their Bible open and pen poised, quietly asking God to reveal himself and his will in every situation. Invariably, there is something they'll read out of the Old Testament history, wisdom literature, or the New Testament that gives them clear direction. They discover the most important adjective of all about the Bible is that it's a living book! It speaks to their needs and makes them open to what God would do.

We've heard it all. When a businessman is praying over an employee situation, a young mother's kids are driving her crazy, a young professional states that she can't stand her boss, or a middle-aged man confesses he can't master pornography in his life, God begins to respond to their honesty with the truth. They have to learn to listen for it. As they grow in their faith, they begin to see God all day long in the everyday events taking place around them.

This happened to me as well and has redefined my life to a large extent. When people start reading their Bibles and journaling like this, the next thing they know, they're worshiping, God is speaking, and they're excited. This is when spending time with God flies instead of creeps by.

Living Sunday to Sunday

We wonder, *Why are so many of our churches dead?* Because our personal worship is dead.

Sunday should be just a bookend on the individual, personal reflection with God we've practiced all week. Instead, in far too many churches, we've turned Sunday into the worship event, and the pastor is the Great Entertainer. I am a diplomat-preacher, and I see it as my job to mobilize the troops to go work, not to come and entertain them where they can't wait to come back and hear me again. My goal is to mobilize an army to change the world. That starts with their own personal interaction with God. No, in fact, it actually starts with my own interaction with God—something I hadn't counted on.

WHEN WILL JESUS BE ENOUGH?

One Monday morning a year into our church's tumultuous move into the renovated shopping center, I got up early to pray in the pasture behind my house (not too unusual in Texas). I was depressed about our unexpected decline. I had heard Rick Warren say that pastors should go somewhere they could plant their lives. Thom Wolf had also noted that in the early church "the pastors stayed and the politicians moved.... If we wanted to change our culture, then we pastors were going to have to stay." I'd made that commitment public many times.

It's a real fun thing to stay when things are going your way, but when they're headed south, well, that's another story. Things at this time were horrible and I wanted to leave. In fact, the only thing keeping me there was my public announcement that I would stay. I had made that statement years earlier, and I always restated it in the New Members Class. My own word had trapped me! Had I not made it publicly, maybe I would have lied to myself and left.

It wasn't as if I hadn't had the opportunity to leave. I listed all the churches and positions I had turned down in order to be faithful to staying at the church. I was half-praying and half-reminding God of my track record. I was in essence telling God how I had held up my end of the bargain and he needed to hold up his. I told God what a good deal he had in me. I had never been unfaithful to my wife (like pastors I knew) or taken money from the offering plate (like stories I'd heard).

I began to think, "If we had had just another hundred people yesterday, I wouldn't be depressed. Why not just another hundred people, God?" I felt so foolish and immature, and I fell on my knees and began to weep. Suddenly, a question came into my mind that has never let me go to this day. God often speaks to me in questions, and the question he posed to me on that day was this, *"Bob, when will Jesus be enough for you?"*

Why Wasn't I Content?

For the first time in my life, I had to admit that Jesus wasn't enough. I loved him and wanted to serve him, but I was too tied up with the ministry and not enough with Jesus. I was more interested in the kingdom of Bob than in the kingdom of God. After that initial query, a torrent of other questions flooded my mind. *Why wasn't*

I content? I had the Holy Spirit and the Word of God; I had experienced salvation and joy; I had a beautiful family and a nice place to live. Nothing was really wrong—I just was not as successful as I thought I should be. *Why didn't I have the peace I was promising all those people who came to hear me speak? What if this was as good as it gets? Why couldn't I be content?*

Something was wrong. I realized how much my ego was tied to my personal success. If Jesus was enough, I had to get over my empire and focus on his kingdom. That day began a love relationship with Christ that has grown into a communion between my heart and his.

How Does Jesus Become Enough?

I believe that before anyone will honestly and consistently fellowship with God, he or she must be convinced that God is enough. One of the Old Testament names for God, El Shaddai, can be translated, "God, the enough."

What does it take to know God as he really is, and why should we get to know him anyway? In the Bible, we see that God does everything for his glory. He longs to fellowship with us in order to reveal his glory to us. It goes back to the reason why we were converted in the first place. We are converted not for ourselves alone but for God—that his glory will be known.

Many people who have never personally interacted with God view him as "The Great Zapper!"—just waiting for people to mess up so he can punish them. Then there are those who think interacting with God merely means showing up on a Sunday morning at church. There are many who feel as if they have tried being with him in the past only to grow angry and bitter if God didn't do what they wanted. G. K. Chesterton wrote, "Christianity has not so much been tried and found wanting, as it has been found difficult and left untried."[1]

If Jesus is enough, what does it mean to know him intimately and live for him even when things are difficult? How is your relationship with God going? Are you able to say with a sincere heart that Jesus is enough for you? I have identified some important keys to Jesus' becoming enough for our lives, our churches, and our world.

Get in a Position to Receive All That He Wants to Give You

For the convert, it is repentance. For the believer, it is self-surrender. For the church, it is engagement outside of itself, not just within and for itself. Jesus has made everything available to us as individuals and to the church corporately if we will only receive it.

First John 3:1 says, "See what love (incredible quality of love) the Father has given (lavished on, bestowed on) us, that we should be called (permitted to be named, counted as) children of God, and so we are" (RSV, parentheses added). As long as we try to make other things enough, we will never be satisfied with the love Jesus lavishes on us. Let's face it: We are not going to get enough from our spouse, kids, friends, and relatives, and definitely not from this world. How do we get to a point where what Jesus has to offer is enough and we don't wonder why he is not enough?

> Praise be to the God and Father of our Lord Jesus Christ, who has blessed us in the heavenly realms with every spiritual blessing in Christ. For he chose us in him before the creation of the world to be holy and blameless in his sight. In love he predestined us to be adopted as his sons through Jesus Christ, in accordance with his pleasure and will—to the praise of his glorious grace, which he has freely given us in the One he loves. In him, we have redemption through his blood, the forgiveness of sins, in accordance with the riches of God's grace that he lavished on us with all wisdom and understanding. And he made known to us the mystery of his will according to his good pleasure, which he purposed in Christ. (Ephesians 1:3–9)

Consider all that this passage says God has done for us. It's all there—total acceptance and total empowerment. What more could God give us? He gave himself; what is left?

If we are not convinced God has given us enough, we will have an incessant need for others to affirm us. We will want others to give us praise, we will crave money, and we will wish to be viewed as the best, the most talented, and the most likely to succeed. Most people never get far beyond their accolades in the high school yearbook. Why? Because they look for what others have to offer to make them feel significant instead of finding their identity in Christ. However, to receive from others, we have to prove ourselves and dance their dance. To be in a position to receive from God, we accept all he has done, just as we are.

Let Go of Your Own Glory and Ego and Embrace God's Glory

There is no better example of this than Moses. He came on the scene in one of those hinge moments in history, but would God be able to do something with him? Moses must have realized dark times call for bright leaders, but could he do it? If we're in it for us, difficulty makes us stop and reconsider. If we're in it for him, we will make it. Missionary Hudson Taylor said, "It doesn't matter how great the pressure is; what really matters is where the pressure lies. Whether it comes between you and God or presses you nearer his heart."[2]

Harsh times don't escape God's notice.

Moses had an inkling of what God was going to do through him, but he initially also had arrogance and pride. He was raised in Pharaoh's court, and because his ego and pride were uncontrolled, his ethics were self-serving and relative to what needed to be done. "The end justifies the means" was his Machiavellian philosophy—so he murdered an Egyptian guard in a rage. But that wasn't God's agenda. God's work must be done in God's way. All our movement is God's work.

Sadly, all too often our sense of significance is tied to the fact that we want what we want and how we want it. D. L. Moody said once that Moses lived his life in three phases. He spent his first forty years thinking he was somebody, his second forty years finding out he was a nobody, and his third forty years discovering what God could do with a nobody! Is there anything wrong with ambition? No, unless it is self-centered. Philippians 2:3 reminds us, "Do nothing out of selfish ambition or vain conceit, but in humility consider others better than yourselves."

See God in Every Circumstance No Matter How Painful or Difficult

Len Sweet tells the story of talking to a seminary graduate who had received job opportunities to be a youth pastor, but nothing else. When Len asked what he was going to do, the student replied, "I don't do youth." To that, Len asked, "What if Michelangelo would have said, 'Sorry, I don't do ceilings?'"

Sometimes the things that bring disappointment and brokenness are the very things God has allowed so he can use them. I am convinced had NorthWood continued on successfully with thousands on our rolls in 1992, I would have never been broken and open to seeing what God wanted to do. He certainly wasn't moving in a way I wanted or expected.

Not long ago, someone asked me if NorthWood was all that I thought it would be by now. I told them in attendance I assumed we would be tens of thousands by now. My wife says I can preach as powerfully as Hybels and Warren—maybe! But in terms of impacting our community, state, nation, and what we're involved in around the world—I had no clue that we would be anywhere near where we are. Lately, we've been brainstorming how NorthWood can plant a hundred churches a year. If each church grew to only a hundred people in the first year, and most will grow beyond, that would be ten thousand people in a single year!

I once heard a woman who had gone through tremendous suffering say, "People ask me how I can handle all the bad things that have happened to me. I tell them that I have always been able to distinguish between bad times and hard times." When the self-centered life has run its course, it will wind up in the desert. But there is always a well nearby! The Hebrew word for desert is *midbar*, which derives from the Hebrew word *dabar*, which means "to speak." If you find yourself in the desert right now, ask God to speak to you in the midst of your circumstances. When life's circumstances turn against us, they produce in us dependence on God and the Christian quality of perseverance. Such dependence in turn teaches patience, and patience makes us wise (cf. Rom. 5:3–5; 2 Cor. 12:7–10).

When we see God in every circumstance, we have to be open and flexible. We have to ignore the present difficulty, knowing something good is coming from it. When we see God, we can listen to him alone. A leader is someone who, while welcoming the friendship and support of others, has sufficient resources to stand alone, even in the face of fierce opposition. He or she must be prepared to have no one but God.

Prepare to Move with God Instead of Holding Onto a Name for Yourself

Abraham, Moses, Jeremiah, Isaiah, Paul, and others were successful, yet they didn't allow their lives to be summed up in one act or one event. Why was this? Because success and failure were relative to the bigger picture.

Many of us would like to be Hebrews 11 kind of people. However, most of them never accomplished their greatest dreams. They moved toward them, and as they did, they achieved more than most ever dream of accomplishing. However, in their lifetimes, they weren't written up in the headlines. Many died without anyone affirming them except God. Scripture says that they saw something better:

> All these people were still living by faith when they died. They did not receive the things promised; they only saw them and welcomed them from a distance. And they admitted that they were aliens and strangers on earth....
>
> These were all commended for their faith, yet none of them received what had been promised. God had planned something better for us so that only together with us would they be made perfect. (Hebrews 11:13, 39–40)

A dream can be accomplished quickly. A vision requires an entire lifetime.

Give God a Lifetime in Which to Work

There is an underlying message in our culture that if we don't hurry and make it to the top quickly, there will be nothing left to celebrate. But once you make it to the top, where do you go? The question is not what did you achieve by what age, but what did you accomplish with your life? Moses didn't let difficulty deter him from his overall mission. He lived by a voice that guided him all the way through his lifetime. To be a Moses, therefore, takes a lifetime. Jesus really is enough for many, many lifetimes over. If our intimate interaction with God empowers us to begin living that, I wonder how we, the church, and the world will be different?

Leadership and management consultant Bobb Biehl has told me many times that if one wants to change the world, plan on at least thirty years. He's right. Churchill said something similar, "Tired old men run the world." It's true. Sure, there are young people out there as world leaders, but the majority of people leading at high levels are those who have been seasoned over time, gained some wisdom, kept their energy, and know how to leverage. This makes life fun. I once heard a speaker say those shooting stars in their twenties and thirties often become falling stars in their forties and fifties. It's one thing to make it big in your field; it's another thing to redefine your field so that you change it and the world!

HOW DO WE INTERACT WITH GOD?

The only way in which we will ever be different is if we are more enamored with the person than we are the process. Transformed people are focused on Jesus—and they are first convinced that he is enough. Then, they are persuaded that time with that person is more important than the actual study.

Jesus said the Pharisees studied the Scripture, yet they failed to see him between the lines. I can tell you how I commune with God, but don't get so caught up in the steps that you miss Jesus. I can teach you how the Christian life is doable and livable in the twenty-first century, but remember it's more caught than taught. Jesus said imitate me. Paul said imitate me. John said imitate me. It's a way of life, not an instruction manual on part assembly. By being near Jesus, living in his presence in a daily manner, we come to know him. How do we enter his presence? Start with honesty.

Honesty Is Primary

God has a beautiful way of putting together what we need just when we need it. Leighton Ford was one of those people God brought into my life for whom I will always be grateful. I had just gone through our church campus relocation and I was still in pain. A great leader and mentor, Leighton had handpicked twenty young men to pour his life into for two years, and I was one of them. He told us he believed that we would all be significant leaders. So, he was bringing us together not so much to make us better leaders as to make us healthier leaders. He wanted us to end our ministry with our mind, morality, marriages, and ministry intact.

At times, he would instruct us to have personal retreats and quiet times to reflect. Not long after I'd begun this journey of transformation, I was on a mountain somewhere in the Carolinas with only my Bible and my journal. As I grew quiet, I began to write about the relationship of faith, hope, love, fear, and idolatry. I realized my obsession was with what I feared and that my idols were the walls I created to protect myself from my fears.

I began to let go of them as I journaled, one at a time, and for the first time in my life came near to the darkness in my own heart. Central to interacting with God is a focus on God's Word and honest confession—brutal honesty being the goal.

Later at another meeting with Leighton, we had to take personality tests. After I received my results, there were things I saw that I didn't like. Truth be told, all of us were pretty depressed. The next morning, feeling frustrated over my own inadequacies, I had breakfast with Leighton and asked him, "Why couldn't I have been more normal like you or your brother-in-law Billy Graham? To be like I am, I hate it!" He looked at me, trying to comfort me, and said, "Bob, do you think Billy and I haven't had our challenges, headaches, and difficulties within ourselves to deal with?" That had never crossed my mind. I had always thought they were leaders because they were gifted and didn't have junk like me. Then it hit me; they were leaders not because they didn't have junk but because they mastered their junk.

Personal transformation starts with deep reflection based on the truth of God's Word and laying your life down beside it, lining it up as a plumb line. Until you master yourself, you have no business trying to master the world. Gordon MacDonald has written: "Many years ago I learned their dirtiest, most crabbed secret. That their passion to change the world derived from the fact that they could not change themselves."[3] This is what reading God's Word with an open journal is all about. It's about slow reflection and moving from thinking in terms of pragmatics to thinking in terms of meaning and significance.

Not long ago, I was speaking at our church on the importance of reflection. A journal is a catalogue of reflections. When you create years of reflective catalogues that tie into what is going on in your life and God's Word, you provide yourself with a way to understand who you are and how God works in your life. You also wind up leaving those you love with a spiritual autobiography of what it's like to wrestle with God — if you're honest.

Daily Time with Him

How does knowing God work? I used to talk about having a quiet time with God where I'd read my Bible and pray my list every day. But it was never passionate and alive on a consistent basis. It seems there were always the ups and downs that came with that mentality. Then I began to discover what personal worship was all about. The Bible, my journal, a pen, perhaps a devotional book, and Starbucks, and I'm good to go.

> *I stopped approaching my "quiet time" as a spiritual positioning activity for the day and began to approach it as an encounter with Christ.*

I deliberately began to change the traditional format—pray first, then read and journal, or journal, read and pray, and journal. More than anything I approached these quiet moments alone with God with the attitude, "Jesus, talk to me, teach me, tell me, convict me, show me, guide me, make your path plain." I would write my deep feelings and concerns. I would read Scripture with a mindset that God was going to speak to me today. I asked myself, "What do I do with what I've read? How do I apply this? How is this going to transform me?" Gradually, other things like meditation, solitude, singing (albeit off-key), and many other disciplines began to make their way into these times.

KEYS TO PERSONAL WORSHIP

I generally experience five critical phases when I am engaged in personal worship—an interactive relationship with God.

Expect God to Show Up

The first phase is a time of invitation and expectation for God to be present. It's where we stop, focus, and listen to what God would say to us. In order for that to happen, we must have a set time and place where we meet God. Jesus knew the power of the place. "And in the morning, rising up a great while before day, he went out, and departed into a solitary place, and there prayed" (Mark 1:35 KJV). It needs to be a place of quietness and inspiration where God can speak. It needs to be a set time with him, where he expects us to show up and we expect the same of him. That place gets us into his place.

> Who shall ascend into the hill of the LORD? or who shall stand in his holy place?
> He that hath clean hands, and a pure heart; who hath not lifted up his soul unto vanity, nor sworn deceitfully. (Psalm 24:3 – 4 KJV)

Focus

Scripture and prayer should be merged, not isolated. And get practical about it. Study a translation of the Bible you can understand. I always have a pen and/or a highlighter nearby when I read the Scripture because I'm not just reading facts. I'm moving from research to application. I'm asking questions such as:

- God, is there something here you're convicting me of?
- God, is there something here you're telling me to do?
- God, are you teaching me something about yourself?
- God, are you giving me a word for something?

When the answer to those kinds of questions comes, I write it in my journal. If it's something super powerful like a life verse or divine direction, I'll also date it and mark it in the margin of my Bible. I would also encourage you to read through the Bible every year, something I've done for the past fifteen years. I've grown more when I read through it every year than any other way. I focus daily on passages in the Old and New Testaments. That strategy keeps me balanced. In fact, after I had read through the Bible a couple of years, I went back to just devotions, and it wasn't nearly as fruitful.

> Thy word is a lamp unto my feet, and a light unto my path. (Psalm 119:105 KJV; see also Psalm 119:1 – 11)

Introspection

Introspection is answering the question, *How will I exemplify what I've learned?* This is where prayer and meditation comes in.

We don't just confess superficial things, but we begin to go deep and focus on the things that cause the sin patterns in our lives. This is also where God speaks in powerful ways about things he wants done. "Search me, O God, and know my heart: try me, and know my thoughts: And see if there be any wicked way in me, and lead me in the way everlasting" (Psalm 139:23–24 KJV). Here's an excerpt from my journal that shows how introspection works:

> 1/26/92 Reality came into my presence kicking and screaming … To see barriers and obstacles that you know you cannot overcome. To give up on the last vestige of hope. Others have gone over the wall. They still do and forever will — but your vaulting pole is just too short, and you don't get to borrow someone else's. We live failing … but don't let it get us down because we know it's just preparation for the big win. What do you do when you realize there will be no big win; settle for only okayness, maybe? Do other people believe and expect as much as I do? I guess each person defines those things.

Inspiration and Exaltation

My journal for the first few years was written on sheets of paper, but I bought a real journal about seven years ago. I chronicle the activities of the day, events that are going on in my life, lessons God is teaching me, and prayer requests. In short, it's not a diary but a running dialogue of my life. When I review it, I can celebrate God's goodness when I see a visible record of his past faithfulness. It inspires me to praise him in advance for the work he will do for me in the future. Having done this now for ten years, I've learned that I can go back, read my journal at the end of the year, and recognize patterns and ways that God is working. Everything God does this year is built on what he began putting together last year.

Journaling allows you to understand how God is working and where he is headed at certain points in your life.

Invigoration and Exercise

The fifth and final stage is invigoration and exercise. I never leave this time without first making a commitment to God. Worship and exercise can be a powerful combination. I often run listening to praise music and worshiping God in my heart. This is another excerpt from my journal that is typical of how I leave my time with God:

> Today is Monday and this day we as a staff are going to spend the day in prayer, evaluation and planning. I've been asking myself, *What would be something worth giving my life to that I could accomplish the next 20 years?* One thing: that from NorthWood a movement would start that would lead to every UPG hearing the Gospel in the next 20 years. God show me how. This week, I expect God to speak.

WHO SAID THIS WAS SUPPOSED TO BE EASY?

"Everyone thinks of changing humanity, no one thinks of changing himself." Leo Tolstoy

The only way we will experience the transformed life Jesus intends for us is if *we embrace discipline.* The Christian experience hinges on the dimension of discipline. And yet some people view grace and discipline as not going together. However, discipline is the root of true discipleship.

Discipline is the believer's response to grace that puts one at the door of grace in order to be transformed. Discipline means planting the seed in the ground so that it can grow. How can we know the depth of grace if we don't spend more time experiencing it? Only discipline allows someone to know God deeply.

Why Is It So Hard to Know God Intimately?

Who said this was all supposed to be so easy? In Romans 7, the apostle Paul had a battle on his hands between what he wanted to do and his flesh. Discipline moves us from contemplating the right choices to doing the right things. Philippians 2:12–13 reminds us, "Therefore, my dear friends, as you have always obeyed—not only in my presence, but now much more in my absence—continue to work out your salvation with fear and trembling, for it is God who works in you to will and to act according to his good purpose."

What is the one thing that the exceptional people who change the world have in common? They live the same twenty-four hours in a day that you and I share, but they live by discipline. Proverbs 5:23 says that people "die for a lack of discipline." We want so much out of God, but offer so little in response.

I've talked to many successful businessmen and women who sacrifice themselves for their jobs in order to gain success. They say they want to learn how to personally interact with God, but they often throw him their calendaring scraps and don't understand why they don't know more about him. There are many things in life we can't control, but one thing we can control is our level of discipline. We do not stop to realize that we are only what we choose to be. We are what we have made ourselves into being. "Superficiality is the curse of our age. The doctrine of instant satisfaction is a primary spiritual problem. The desperate need today is not for a greater number of intelligent people, or gifted people, but for deep people."[4]

If we are not willing to be disciplined, our lives will not be near what they could be in any and every dimension. Proverbs 10:17 says, "He who heeds discipline shows the way to life." Most of us want to play in the game, but they don't want the workout required. Do you want victory in your life? Do you want to do something significant? The key is not whom you know, or even how much you desire significance. The key is discipline. Only those who significantly discipline their lives will ever do anything worthwhile or grow as a person.

How Much of God?

However, too often we just simply don't care. We want just enough God to make us nice, just enough God to be respectable, just enough God for people to think well of us. There are no three easy steps to changing our mentality and incorporating discipline into our lives, only many hard steps. "It costs a man just as much or even more to go to hell than to come to heaven. Narrow, exceedingly narrow is the way to perdition!"[5] People who live disciplined lives are looking at maximum sacrifice for maximum result. They want impact. It isn't about beating someone else; it's about being the best that you can be.

How much of God do you have in your life? I can tell you: As much as you want.

WHY INTERACT WITH GOD?

T-Life begins and ends on this first step—practicing an interactive relationship with God. We will not be transformed people apart from our intimate fellowship with God. We will never change the world if we do not first change ourselves. For a church that's been called to tackle the world, she must first tackle herself. E. Stanley Jones says that the reason the apostles could turn the world upside down is that they first mastered the most difficult place, Jerusalem.[6] If it would work there, it would work anywhere. Then they moved out to the ends of the earth. Had they not tackled Jerusalem, they probably wouldn't have reached the world. However, they reached Jerusalem, and they did so because they mastered themselves.

Intimate, interactive communion with God must become core to who we are or else we will not progress as individuals or as the church. But if we as individuals begin to practice the presence of God (as Brother Lawrence would say), we will begin to seek connections with other like-minded believers.

That's where it really gets exciting. We will have moved from the individual to life upon life. That's why the next component in the T-Life moves us from interacting with God to interacting with one another in ways that involve transparency and accountability for authentic Christian living. What this spiritual synergy of transformed people produces is far more superior and longer lasting than anything else we do in this life as individuals. Connection keeps our own personal walk with God from being private, and it keeps us from escaping the reality check that accountability provides.

QUESTIONS TO THINK ABOUT AND TALK ABOUT

1. Is Jesus enough for you? Explain. What behavior or attitudes demonstrate we believe he is or is not enough for us?

2. How do you read the Bible? Describe your practices. What works for you and what is difficult?

3. What otherwise ordinary opportunities, events, and relationships could become extraordinary if you began recognizing God's hand in them?

4. What do you think are the top five benefits of journaling?

Five

CAN FOLLOWING JESUS EVER BE PRIVATE?

Transparent connections
people who are learning to interact with God making
authentic connections with other believers

I had been in Australia, and after the plane landed I walked down the Jetway from the plane heading toward the gate, anxious to see my wife and family waiting for me (remember the pre–9/11 days?). I saw my wife first, and I embraced her and hugged my son and my daughter as tightly as I could. Standing next to them in an awkward way was Ti, the Buddhist/atheist student who had come to live with us. Although I'd heard about his housewarming gifts, we had not yet met. He was petrified because he was now living with a pastor.

So, here he is standing at the airport meeting me for the first time, freaking out and thinking to himself, "I'm going to go to jail when I go back home." When I saw him standing there with his hands in his pockets so scared I just spontaneously hugged him too. He lived with us in our home for two years. He's not accepted Christ … yet … but he's connected with other believers. He is not on his spiritual discovery alone.

I don't know of anything more radical than to bring someone into your home who believes the opposite of what you believe and live it out in front of them. It wasn't easy—and at times still isn't—but Ti has become a part of our family. It's connected us more as a family because he will ask questions he doesn't know he isn't supposed to ask or he will challenge our way of thinking. It has reminded me that healthy families and communities communicate. Church members must communicate and connect in order to grow and serve God. It was never meant to be a lone ranger approach.

So far, almost sixty kids from non-Western nations have lived with members of NorthWood. Eight of the kids who have since come to live with members of our church have accepted Christ and have made strong connections with other believers. And great stuff is happening. All of them are at major universities, doing incredibly well. It is exciting as they email me, call or visit, and tell me how their lives are being blessed with opportunities to work and to serve God. They're doing it all in the context of their life and culture. God has allowed me to meet with educators, businessmen, Supreme Court judges, prime ministers, warlords, and the like. It's not because we found a way to get in the door. It's because our laypeople are transformed and people want to get to know them personally.

CONNECTION DIFFERS FROM COMMUNITY

Community means so many different things to people. The word itself means "common unity." However, there is no unity in the church as a whole today, which is why I prefer the word "connection." I think the church has confused community with socialization. Baboons socialize—they pick the fleas and ticks off one another and play. So what is different about the churches' "community" today as opposed to what we see in a baboon community? It should be the mission that we are on that connects us together.

When Christians in the early church accepted Christ, it was inconceivable that they would accept Christ and not tie in with community (which was defined as the church). How tragic it is that church for some people has merely become a Christian's religious rituals on Sunday morning, not the locus of transparency, authenticity, and accountability that connection provides.

When a church is firing on all three pistons of a transformed life, all hell breaks loose. At least that's what has happened at our church. Last year, we waved good-bye to about seventy-five families out of our church, but we still grew in the area of authentic connections because about four hundred more new people are now part of our church. And they're not just church members. In fact, to be a member of our church, you have to be in a small group. Eighty percent of our entire attendance is involved in small groups of Bible study and prayer because we've learned that there is no accountability outside of community.

We're not living it until we sit down with one another and ask the hard questions.

CONNECTION IS CRUCIAL

I dreaded the meeting. Andy Williams, a close friend and staff member at that time, came in my office and told me something I didn't want to hear. One of our church planters had a problem with pornography. His wife had caught him once. He said it was a fluke and would never happen again. Still, other areas of his life were totally out of control, which is not abnormal for addictive behaviors. Financially, physically, morally, he was out of control and needed help.

There were many questions with other areas of his ministry that began to surface. I met with him and his wife and told them we'd help them and stand beside them, but he needed to step down. It was a horrible experience. He was ready, but his wife wasn't. She had experienced her own difficult childhood, and now all the security that she had acquired was being destroyed. Two weeks later, Andy and I went to be there when he stepped down. Sadly, the church didn't survive—there really is something about leadership and health.

The young couple involved moved over to our area, rented a home, and started going to NorthWood. They were in counseling, went to some retreats, plugged into a small group, and begin to start recovery. They also both got secular jobs and started putting their lives back together. It wasn't easy for them. But they both submitted to what we asked them to do, even though they didn't like it at times.

Jordon Fowler, our worship pastor, and I were working on our preaching plan that year. We began to read all the stats on people in the ministry dealing with pornography. We talked about doing a sermon series on it, but then we thought it might be too controversial. I wanted to call it "Porno — A little dab will doom ya," but we wound up calling it "PorNo." We decided if it was that big in the ministry, what must it be doing to our laypeople in the pews?

We took a gamble and even did a mass mailer. Obviously, "religious" people didn't like it, so we got a few calls on that one. However, the church was packed out, and it is still one of the most successful teaching series we've ever done. We had a psychologist and someone who had come out of the addiction, as well as a lady who survived her husband's addiction. It was powerful. We announced we were starting a support group. We didn't know if anyone would sign up — man, were we wrong. We have had several of these groups now, and the leader for the first one was none other than the young church planter who came out of his addiction. He's told his story, and it's been amazing. He has had a huge impact and after three years is getting ready to enter back into vocational ministry. There is hope.

A Place to Deal with Life

We've discovered that it is absolutely essential in discipleship to have many kinds of groups. Talking about pornography or various addictions can be difficult in a typical small group, but if someone wants to tackle those issues, we must have a place for them to deal with it. "If you have an addiction, we have a place for you," I like to say. Each year, we now deal with at least two series on mental and emotional health. I used to believe "all they needed was Jesus," but when I came to see transformation as the changing of character, then it wasn't just about emotional "issues," it became central to discipleship.

Other groups like Crown Financial Freedom, or Neil Cole's LTG (Life Transformation Groups), men's groups, women's groups, and so on are all essential so that people can deal with the issues they are facing. Hundreds of people have gone through our support groups because if we want to plant churches that change our community and engage the world, we must have people who are mastering themselves. Some of these people coming out of our groups make our best transformers in a glocal setting.

PERSONAL BUT NEVER PRIVATE

Hebrews 12:1 – 3 gives us a picture of connection:

> Therefore, since we are surrounded by such a great cloud of witnesses, let us throw off everything that hinders and the sin that so easily entangles, and let us run with perseverance the race marked out for us. Let us fix our eyes on Jesus, the author and perfector of our faith, who for the joy set before him endured the cross, scorning its shame, and sat down at the right hand of the throne of God. Consider him who endured such opposition from sinful men, so that you will not grow weary and lose heart.

This picture of inspiring examples reminds us that no one runs in isolation. I used to think Jesus and I could handle anything alone, but that is not true. We need the whole body of Christ. Only Jesus saves, and only Jesus keeps — but he puts us in community to grow and develop, not in isolation. In other words, there is a reason why God created the church. We were created to live in community. We have been instructed not to forsake the assembling of ourselves together. We were born into the community of the kingdom and the local church is the seed bed that we live in together.

Our conversion is personal, but never private.

Imitate Me

To our own demise, we have so idealized the "Christian" life and perspective that we fail to believe that it really is livable. Why is that? Because so few are living it as it is intended to be lived. Therefore, we come to consider it a noble idea, a good thing to strive for, but certainly not obtainable. If it were, we'd see more people doing it.

Yet when we read about Paul and others, it becomes plain that not only was it doable, but it was done. This Christian life can be and has been lived. It can be and is being lived. It is more than a noble idea and more than an aspiration; it is an expectation of all believers.

Paul says to "mimic" me, Solomon instructs his son in Proverbs to "do as he does." What a powerful statement! How many of us can say, "Do it like me and you'll do it right"? Some might say this is arrogant, but that is only if Paul's life did not back up his words. When he said "mimic" me, he was saying, "I've lived around you and near you; what you have seen me live, you live." And we know they did (Acts 20:18). Living out the Christian life gives value to the experience—to you and to the "cloud of witnesses" who are watching you.

CONNECTION HELPS US WITH OUR CALL

We must move from an individual's call to change the world to more of a corporate, communal, congregational call to the world. To most church people, church means a shelter, a place to have friends and to find encouragement and support. However, shouldn't it be more than that? We've not explored the exponential power of transformed lives to its fullest extent. Researchers have discovered that teamwork only results when people have an overarching goal to accomplish that (1) requires everyone and (2) reflects on everyone.[1] However, when teamwork is focused on itself for the sake of team building, it rarely happens. A task that goes far beyond just ourselves pulls us together to create a sense of support and authentic connection.

However, American individualism praises the person who does it on his or her own, his or her own way. Our culture celebrates the lone rangers instead of reining the mavericks into community. As independent, aggressive, and intense as Paul appears to have been as an individual, even he voluntarily lived in the context of community. I believe one reason why the church is exploding in Asia is that it doesn't have this individualistic, self-centered concept as the West does. Ho Chi Minh in the early days of socialism in Vietnam challenged Russian communist leaders not to ignore Asia. He predicted that communism would even do better there than in the West because people lived in more of a "community" mindset. He was right.

The message of Christianity centers on the cross on which Christ died. Every believer helps one another carry his or her own cross. In the West, the message of Christianity is likened to a personal secret discovery like a fountain of youth or lucky penny. If I accept Jesus as my God, not necessarily my Lord, then he will get me everything I want. Connection helps break us of that individualistic, selfish mentality so that we see others around us who need our encouragement and vice versa.

Connecting in community allows us to serve together and make a difference together.

CONNECTION REFLECTS THE KINGDOM

Connection with other believers is important because it is the context for which we are to live out the Christian life in accountability. It is important because together is the only way we can ever accomplish the fulfillment of the Great Commission. It is important because it says everyone is important, yet it breaks us of individualism. Connection with other believers is important because it reflects as the earthly kingdom of God the future kingdom of God in heaven.

The greatest obstacle of the church in America is not the onslaught from without, but the fighting from within.

No aspect of the kingdom of God is as essential as how we get along together. If we are not united, our voice will be silenced, our message will be weakened, our influence nonexistent, and our fellowship fractured. Yet this is the state of the church today. People today jump from church to church for two reasons: They want to find people who agree with them or who will tolerate their sin.

Of all the metaphors that Jesus chose to expound upon, he picked the notion of kingdom, which in and of itself connotes community. Not only did Jesus promise he would never leave us nor forsake us, but he also built a community where we would be there for one another. He makes us into a body, as Paul wrote in 1 Corinthians 12. However, from the start, we have erected as quick as we can walls, camps, and favorite leaders, thus fragmenting the body without a single voice or powerful impact. Yet Jesus said the world would know us by one thing only: our love for one another. Did he mean that? Many seemingly good people seem to doubt it when they are on opposite sides of issues fighting with one another.

A MODEL OF CONNECTION

One year, I preached on nothing but the Sermon on the Mount, the point being that if a person were in a transforming mode, he or she would practice making transparent connections in small groups for accountability, ministry, journaling, evangelism, and prayer. We then have what's called NorthWood Notes during the week to help people throughout the week process in practical ways what they have heard on Sunday morning. The majority of our small groups—what we call teams—follow the notes in a corporate, small group kind of setting. Our goal is to make a seamless transition between evangelism and discipleship.

We must progress in the model from an *interactive relationship with God* to *transparent connections with others* and on to the hard work of Glocal Impact—applying all that we know in real time. From the inner life to its outward expression in service.

Mike had always been "religious," but when he grew older, he got away from it. His best friend lost his brother. At the funeral, he heard Randy Miller speak, one of the NorthWood pastors, and decided to visit our church. Within a few months, he gave his heart to Christ and was baptized. He began to get involved in a small group, then youth ministry, then his wife and daughter went overseas on a trip with NorthWood. On his fortieth birthday, vacationing in Cancun in shallow water, a wave knocked him down and broke his neck. On exactly the fourth year to the day he was baptized, we were having his funeral in our worship center. Many people were there who had visited NorthWood at Mike's invitation. Many had seen the transformation in Mike's life. Within a month, several of those people accepted Christ and were baptized.

Recently, as I was preaching in our service I saw three men there as a result of Mike living a changed life before them. Some of those he influenced are in small groups and some are in support groups and some are just trying to get on their feet. But it was a life that worked for Mike in the context of community that they want and they are obtaining. There was nothing lone ranger about Mike's faith.

QUESTIONS TO THINK ABOUT AND TALK ABOUT

1. Why is it so hard to be radically transparent with people?
2. What are four benefits of being in a "group" community?
3. What are the top reasons people give for not being in a group?
4. "Jesus and I can handle anything alone." Do you agree or disagree? Why?

Six

WHAT IF THE CHURCH WERE THE MISSIONARY?

Glocal impact
convergence of life, ministry, and vocation —
the bridge between a person's vocation and ministry
that spans community development locally and globally

O h no, God, don't let me go to sleep." That's the last prayer I expected to pray while in a room with Leighton Ford and other key American religious leaders as they challenged us toward evangelism. He was leading a conference at Southwestern Seminary and needed some grunt help, so I volunteered. My home is only thirty minutes away, so I could still work at the church office up until the last minute of the conference and then head over. After a full day working, I was tired when the conference began that evening—by dimming the lights to show a film.

Fortunately, I was on the edge of my seat instead of on the verge of sleep by the time the opening credits rolled for a film focused on the Unreached People Groups (UPGs) of the world. There are entire cultures that have never had a chance at the gospel, billions of people who have never even heard the name of Jesus Christ. As I listened, my heart quickened.

When I graduated from seminary, the first thing my wife and I did was to apply to be foreign missionaries. Ever since I was a child, I felt as if I was headed overseas. For a number of reasons, it didn't work out, and I was terribly disappointed. I had taken extra classes in missions because I thought I'd be a missionary. I wouldn't even marry Nikki until I knew for sure she would be open to living as a missionary. On two other occasions after that, we tried again, but it never came together for us.

When the conference was over that night, I was upset as I drove home. Staring out my windshield, I told God, "You know I'm willing. I have three degrees. I'm educated, I'm a risk taker, and I want to go. Yet you've not allowed me to be a missionary. Why would you have me sit through all of that tonight? I'd go, but I can't go!" Silence filled the air, and I continued on disappointed and bitter.

The next morning when I got up, I was still griping at God on my way to work. However, this time he spoke to me in another powerful way. By this time, I was pastoring at NorthWood and having a real impact as a result of Jesus finally being enough for me. We had begun planting several churches stateside in response to a renewed vision we had for how the church should be. It was as if he said, "Bob, you've thought about pastoring the church and the kingdom in different ways. Now I want you to think about missions in a different way." Then another question came into my mind that changed the direction of our church and my understanding of kingdom expansion: "What if the church were the missionary?"

READY TO SERVE GOD

This led to the whole concept of Glocal Impact, the third corner on the triangle of the transformed life. Once there is an interactive relationship with God and we are living in community for accountability and relationships with others, then we are ready to serve God. Some people have actually come to NorthWood because of stories they've heard in the news about the glocal impact our church is making and they want to be a part of the action.

Glocal impact is where we challenge every member to serve the community locally and globally.

We want every member to be involved in both geographies. This dual focus is to help them understand God's call on their life for his world, how Christians should make the world different, and how they should use their vocation to make it happen. We see huge spiritual growth here when people begin to engage it. From this also comes our church planting. Ironically, we didn't plant nearly as many churches in the States before we began to connect with the rest of the world.

OLD TIME RELIGION

Historically, the role of local churches in missions has been to pray for the lost of the world and to give the missionaries money. On occasion, if a church was lucky, maybe a young couple would surrender to be missionaries and go somewhere in the world. Church members would keep up with them by notices in the bulletin here and there, but eventually they would lose touch. Some churches were really radical and would send people on a mission trip somewhere in the world. But for the most part, those trips became potential burdens to the missionaries and only great Kodak moments for the participants. Other than making Western Christians feel good about themselves, they had no real impact on the kingdom or cultures.

In addition, there were the mission-minded churches that set a huge goal for world missions each Christmas, complete with guest missionaries who spoke (and most of the time they were boring). This was called being *mission-minded*. I hate that term—mission is much more like being kingdom-engaged. It is an outgrowth of living the kingdom, not an add-on to one of many things the church does; it's what the church is. There were organizations (and still are) for men and women, boys and girls, designed to educate people about missions around the world. However, the concept of the mobilization of a local church to do missions is about as foreign in my tribe as infant sprinkling! Furthermore, outside of that annual emphasis, missions was out of sight and out of mind.

Here's how missions worked in my background. The pastor stood up and pushed for money (he wanted to be considered mission-minded). The money was then sent to the denominational headquarters and from there it was sent to the Foreign Mission Board and on to different countries. From the country, it made its way to the missionary. Finally, from the missionary it made its way to the nationals. Get the idea? That process is so far removed from where the average person lives that there is no way they could understand the need, the world, or the commission.

However, that process was exactly what I was following; it's all I knew. I will never forget in the first year of our church when we were taking up the world missions offering, called the Lottie Moon Christmas Offering. It was in honor of a famous Southern Baptist missionary who starved to death in China. I stood up and passionately gave the plea to give to the Lottie Moon Offering. An unchurched person who happened to also be our neighbor leaned over to my wife and whispered, "Who is Lottie Moon?"

My wife said, "She's a missionary who died many years ago."

In complete sincerity, our neighbor then asked, "Are they trying to raise money to bring her body back?"

I began to realize at that point that our hallowed heroes from other generations (often long forgotten) do not motivate young believers. We need new heroes that others can see and touch in order to realize missions isn't old-time religion but something that requires the whole church today—if it is going to happen at all.

IS THIS WHY I'M HERE?

The question, "What if the church were the missionary?" was so overwhelming when it came to me, I had to pull off the road. It was as if a bomb had just exploded in my mind. I began to weep and ask, "Oh God, is this why you kept me in the pastorate? Is this what I am here for?" Once again, other questions came to me in succession. Wasn't the Great Commission given to the local church? What would it look like if missions became a core component of a church?

What little by that point I had learned about the kingdom of God began to make sense and even connect with this new dimension of local churches being missionaries, not just doing a few mission trips.

How could a church be a missionary? I reasoned over the next few days. I started with the definition of a missionary. Obviously, a person is a missionary because he or she is going to people with little or no access to the gospel to tell the message of Christ and see them come to faith and help them grow. So, could a church do that?

What does a missionary take with them? They take the Word of God, the love of the people, and a love of Jesus to do whatever it takes to reach the people. What would the church take with them?

To whom does the Great Commission belong? Does it belong to a denomination? Missionaries? Mission agencies? I began to understand that the Great Commission belongs to the local church as a whole. My idea wasn't innovative—it was the way it was originally intended to be! That's when I concluded that the Great Commission is local-church given and therefore local-church driven. How does a local church recapture that sense of corporate responsibility? One thing I knew for sure, typical missions education and awareness didn't mobilize any church to go into the world (other than to make them aware that people outside our borders needed God). So how would a church do this? I began to toy with an idea: What would it look like if NorthWood adopted an entire nation, say, China?

Now I was having fun, trying to imagine how a church could do that. I began to think of ways that it could. Specifically, I began to think in terms of Glocal Impact—an interactive relationship between our vocations and ministry that would enable us to impact the world both locally and globally. As our gifts, abilities, and vocations converged with our passion to change the world, the natural outflow would be evident. A church of believers would make a practical, visible difference in the world—with no strings attached because they were in it for the long haul. We would develop discipleship not at a desk with a fill-in-the-blank notebook, but in a context of service and ministry, responding to opportunities that God put in front of us. That's how we would do it.

MODEL OF T-LIFE

The only way we will ever be different is if transformational living becomes an interactive dynamic process. The three different components of the T-Life model are akin to spokes on a wheel—they are in constant motion.

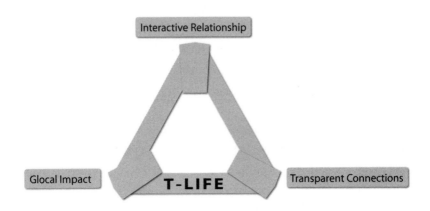

Not steps one, two, three, but more like a cycle whose momentum and energy fuels the transformation through the Holy Spirit. The church, to some degree, has done Interactive Relationship with God and to some degree, it's done Transparent Connections. However, we've often made the biggest mistake at the point of Glocal Impact: convergence with our life and work. We thought we could pay people to be missionaries. But I submit to you that the church is the missionary—every single member.

Missions Mobilization

If the Great Commission was a call on the entire church, then the entire church needed to be involved, but it was going to have to be involved differently than in the past. Why couldn't the missions heroes be modern day nonvocational missionaries? Local church people who went, worked, and returned? Stories not written in books, but stories sitting in the pew beside us? I quickly became convinced that the church is the primary missions agency, not just in the giving of funds as we have in the past, but in the actual "going." Not just involved in prayer but in deployment and strategy.

The visible church lost her supremacy in world missions because she abdicated what God had called her to do. She made the call something only for a very select group or individual. For the rest of us left behind, prayer was an easy and spiritual excuse. Giving was a somewhat painless response—an exercise to convince us we had done our part. Now suddenly, we were in the process of making a quantum leap from missions education to missions mobilization.

The church is the body of Christ moving in the world in the name of Christ—representing him, calling people to him, living and sharing his truth, and through him healing the world's wounds. Now the question becomes, how do we mobilize the church to move out into the world, not just a few but the masses?

Not long after I began to think about the church being a missionary, I began to realize that that had huge implications not just for the role of the church but for the role of the laity as well. I began to wonder how many people like me felt as children they would become missionaries but for one reason or another things hadn't worked out that way. I already knew of a couple in our church in that category.

There can be no doubt; the vehicle for the expansion of the kingdom of God is the church.

So on a whim one Sunday morning I asked each service, "How many of you felt like God was calling you to be a missionary when you were a child or teenager? How many of you would say you seriously considered it, if only for a brief time?" To my utter amazement, over a third of the people lifted their hands. That was significant, given two-thirds of our church was from unchurched backgrounds. I began to wonder, *Could that just be a fluke? How could so many have felt that way? What if God spoke to them years earlier in preparation for something new he was going to do in the future? Something unlike anything the church has seen since the early church?*

WHAT IF GOD REALLY DID CALL THEM?

I seriously begin to ask myself, *What if God really had called them? Furthermore, what if he really also wanted them to work at IBM or Mobil, become doctors, lawyers, businesspersons, and many other occupations? What if God was doing something that we couldn't see a couple of decades ago in calling these people?* The typical response to a child saying he or she was going to be a missionary was, "Well, isn't that sweet!" What if we should instead say, "Well, isn't that God!"

The first-century church exploded as it dispersed because of persecution from the Jewish leaders and the Romans. As Christian businesspeople traveled the transportation routes, the gospel would take root in individual trading cities. So, I asked myself, what was the common language and communication we have today? I realized it was the same as the early church — the business climate. Knowing the world was going to change dramatically and a new world order would focus on the business and information exchange, what if God were placing his soldiers all throughout the structures that would cross nations and ethnicities and be present in every culture? If God were indeed doing that, the great challenge was if the church would recognize it or would instead continue doing missions the same way it has since 1792!

That's when the idea of convergence began to crystallize in my mind. Since I was leading my church to consider going into closed places where traditional missionaries could not go, the laypeople's jobs and backgrounds were better suited than anyone else to do mission work.

> *There are countries in the world you can't go as a missionary. But, you can go as a businessperson, a doctor, a teacher, a humanitarian, and a thousand other things to help that country.*

What is so sad is that some missionaries today are trying to be the businesspeople and merchants that they *are not* in order that they can go places where the real businesspeople in our churches *already are!* Despite what you may have heard, there are no "closed countries." Churches are full of people already in those realms through the information and technological exchange of their jobs and need only to know how to share their faith. Not only were these people called, but also they were best suited to accomplish what God had called them to do.

Unlike Anything the World Has Seen

I then became convinced God had indeed called them and was raising up a new missions force in the world. In the past, most of the "new" with regard to missions has been strategy, but converging an individual's job with ministry opportunities extends beyond strategy to the missions force and personnel itself. Globalization has transformed the role of the laity and opened the door for a radically new missionary force unlike the world has seen since the first-century church.

It is time for the church to set out for the hard places. It is time for the church to redefine what "missions" activity is. Too much of our mission work today has to do with making us feel good about where we go and what we do. We go where it is easy and where we can do what we want to do. But does it make a genuine difference in the world? By contrast, the places that need us the most will require us to respond in different ways:

- You will *not* be allowed to build church buildings.
- You will *not* be allowed to teach Bible studies.

- You will *not* be allowed to pass out tracts.
- You will *not* be allowed to do backyard Bible clubs.
- You *will be allowed* to bring skills to help in nation building, and in those relationships, you will be able to share your faith one on one.

The general response at that point is, "Well, that's not missions!" Welcome to the first-century church. Evangelism is being reduced to individual relationships by travelers around the world like Philip and the Ethiopian eunuch. It will work. The New Testament tells us how!

FROM SHIPS TO MICROCHIPS

People often ask if I believe in "missionaries" anymore. Considering twelve couples have come out of our church so far to be vocational missionaries, that should answer the question. However, more than connecting to an agency or denomination, if I were a missionary I would connect with a church that loved the people I was working with as much as I did.

Globalization combined with what I term *kingdomization* is calling for a new metaphor from "missionary" to kingdom pilgrim. Transformation is not instantaneous; it is a process—a pilgrim journey. And it isn't entirely mission. On a mission, you give; on a pilgrimage, you give and get. We are pilgrims because this isn't our home; we are passing through as we learn to know God and love others. It's a journey because it is a relationship. Living for the kingdom means being pilgrims, learning and enjoying the journey with God.

I believe God is in the process of raising up a completely new breed of kingdom pilgrim that looks different from what we've known in the past. For the past two hundred years, missions has been done the same way as the advent of William Carey. An individual lives in a country his or her entire life to do the work of the mission while the people passively receive it and help spread it to their friends. That was the only way possible when ocean ships were the chief form of travel, exploration, and connecting people.

However, we have moved from ocean ships to microchips, where education and information is far more accessible to every country and every culture. The internet alone has exposed people in different cultures and countries to what life is like across the globe. We are no longer in closed environments using the best of Western civilization to get there. We have to remember that East and West have met and are merging. They may be poor, but they are not ignorant nor are they dependent on us. As a matter of fact, the church in China has done incredibly well without us.

The world is no longer white (if it ever was); the sooner we realize that, the better off we'll be.

HELPING PEOPLE UNDERSTAND GLOCAL IMPACT

If our goal is to turn laypeople in our churches into the new missions force of kingdom pilgrims, we are going to have to develop new ways to process these people in order for them to be effective. At a recent new members class, I went around the room and asked each person what his or her job or vocation was. I have fun explaining how they can use their job to make a difference in the world. We help them find somewhere to plug in here and serve, as well as to find some way to plug into the world and serve. They need to live in both dimensions, local and global. It's what we call *glocal*. They need to do evangelism and discipleship. Our emphasis on "which of these either/ors is the most important" only points to our sickness, not our success. The church is the ultimate both/and. It is the seamless ministry of here and there, secular and sacred, evangelism and discipleship, and hundreds of other examples.

Merge the two components of T-Life—Interactive Relationship with God and Transparent Connections—with the third element of Glocal Impact and you have the elements that started us on this journey. I sure wasn't smart enough to figure it out. God showed us all of those elements had to be there. Had one been missing, we would not be doing what we are today.

How these elements link together in T-Life makes sense when we look at Paul. He was the greatest theologian of the New Testament—and a mystic who knew Christ intimately. However, he was also the greatest missionary of the New Testament and early church. That's why he led others so beautifully. He taught by his example that it wasn't a destination that mattered, it was a life hid in Christ being propelled to the ends of the earth and eternity.

WHY T-LIFE?

A man I would consider the godliest and holiest man in our church went to Vietnam after years of putting it off. He had never been open to going overseas and working with internationals. In fact, he viewed it as something that God would call others to do—certainly not him, and he had a whole list of excuses to prove it. Imagine my surprise when he finally went to Vietnam with a few others from our church. When he returned, I spontaneously asked him to speak about his experience in front of the church.

"Did it make that much difference in you?" I asked.

Our conversation was unrehearsed, but he didn't hesitate when he told our congregation, "It was one of the greatest learning and growing experiences I've ever had in my life."

"Do you feel like you gained some ground in your own personal discipleship?" I then asked him. Many people would have had evangelism on the brain and how much good he was able to do for the other people. But I wanted to know if it improved *his* life.

"Oh, yes!" he agreed heartily.

Our goal is to create an atmosphere where people can hear God and then have the courage to obey him. Now the church is being redefined, not from external bells and whistles but from the internal transformation of the very character of people. The church winds up growing and making an impact based on substance, not hype.

Therefore, the result is not only that people are growing internally, but also as they obey God and follow his will, the church is growing externally.

> *The message we take to transform the world is only as strong as the transformation that has first taken place within us.*

Have You Been Transformed?

What in the world does personal transformation have to do with extending the kingdom of God and missions? Everything! The question is not, *Have you been baptized, converted, or joined a church?* The question is, *Have you been transformed?* We cannot separate the spirituality, moral character, and integrity of the one delivering the message from the message.

People think we do "missions" for the world. That's a false understanding. God is in charge of the world and will work with or without us. Missions is primarily about discipleship. Something happens that changes individuals in a local church when they begin to connect globally. Furthermore, I believe the best hope for the Western church is to engage the world because that is where God is working.

They Can Go Anywhere in the World

I am grateful for what William Carey did in 1792 by being the first "modern" missionary. But we took the Great Commission and turned it into a vocation instead of marching orders for the entire church. In the 1800s, missions was the story of biography. In the 1900s, it was the story of institutions and parachurch groups. But the story of missions today is the laypeople in the pew. They are not waiting for mission boards, mission agencies, or lethargic churches to process them. They're going. I'm meeting them all over the world.

When people start putting their hands on T-life locally in the community, they realize that their job is just as much a calling from God to be a dentist as for me to be a pastor. They are free. They can go anywhere in the world.

GLOCAL IMPACT IN ACTION

A young lady in our church named Jessica died from mental illness. She was a sweet and precious woman who loved going to the children's classes. Several people whom she had impacted began to think about what they could do to touch special needs children. The first thing they did was to start a special needs class for our children's ministry on Sunday mornings. Then they began to think about similar needs in the community. Before long, they came up with a plan, based on Joni Eareckson Tada's material, to host a night for special needs children so their parents could have a "night off" together. We staffed it with our own volunteer doctors, nurses, and many others.

After word got out regarding that successful event, some more special needs adults heard about our ministry. Their director wanted to know if they could come to our worship services. We now have thirty adults that come to the service and over two hundred children. A few months ago, one of these sweet individuals became really loud and a little out of control, as sometimes happens with special needs children. I stopped preaching and told everyone in the service, "Don't worry! They are some of our special friends and we love them." The whole church clapped for them.

Here is where the local impact started to go global. Some of the workers who wrote a curriculum for our church were involved in special needs classes in public schools. They came together and asked if they could use their skills overseas in the nation our church has adopted.

As God would have it, we soon wound up meeting the person in charge of all special needs education on a trip there. This person told us how the special needs children had been mainstreamed—but there was no training for the teachers in the public schools. Our members wrote the curriculum alongside our overseas contact, and a group of fifteen then went to this nation to teach professors and teachers in the entire nation how to effectively mainstream special needs children in their public schools. The next thing we know, we're writing curricula for special needs children across town and across the globe!

When this happens, get ready; the world is about to change because it moves from your church to the Church and beyond.

QUESTIONS TO THINK ABOUT AND TALK ABOUT

1. Have you ever thought or dreamed about being a missionary? Describe what you dreamed.

2. What if you stayed at your current job and you used that job to engage a nation, what would it look like?

3. List six good reasons why your church can't adopt a nation?

4. How would the early church have responded to those six reasons?

Part Three

T-WORLD:

Creating a Church for Transformation

Transformation is possible because we are in an interactive relationship with God, accountable with other believers, and responding to ministry opportunities. The result is that we are living the incarnational life of Christ around those who know us. The vision for significance moves from something just for you personally to being something that you are aspiring to beyond yourself.

Do you see the picture? It's impossible to separate your inner-life growth from an outer-life expression. That's why the *Transformed Life* is in the context of what I call a *Transformed World*. Glocal impact, using one's job and ministry opportunities, is the bridge between the two.

T-World is a vision of every believer and every church engaging the world with the purpose of making a lasting difference. T-World is what the church looks like when it is producing transformed disciples. The early church transformed a world steeped in plurality, immorality, and poverty (much like today) in miraculous ways. How? People lived transformed lives for the world to see; they impacted the church, community, and eventually the whole world.

When the church is fulfilling its purpose, the following three components of T-World will happen simultaneously:

Community development: integral involvement in the community culture and morality

Church multiplication: transformed individuals who make up healthy churches that, in turn, naturally grow and multiply

Nation building: leveraging natural infrastructures for maximum global impact

HOW DO T-LIFE AND T-WORLD FIT TOGETHER?

People often ask me, "How do you get to where you are? How does it all fit together?" The six components of T-Life and T-World may seem unrelated at first. However, they all relate in the big picture. Don't look at these areas as individual specialties from which you can pick and choose. That's not how it works! Seeing the whole is essential to understanding how the kingdom of God works. The kingdom is the ultimate convergence of all domains.

However, we've segmented how God works—and we've done so to our own detriment. Only when we see the bigger picture of how the pieces fit together can there be any flow or continuity. I call this way of learning *domain jumping*.[1] In other words, instead of learning and

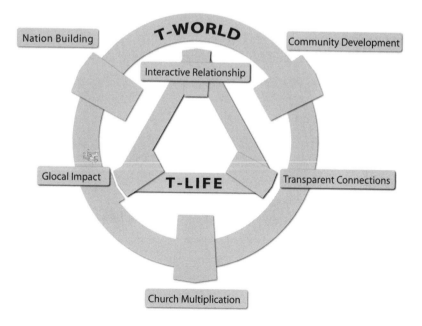

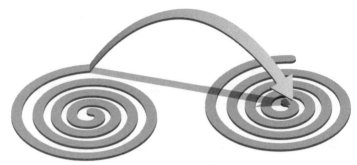

Domain Jumping   Figure 2

mastering only one domain or specialty for a lifetime, we allow one domain to naturally lead to learning in the next related domain. We're curious. We want to know how it all relates instead of camping out on only one domain. It's the difference between learning sequentially or in a cumulative pattern and making a beeline from the big picture outward to master a domain of information (see figure above). Curiosity drives this kind of learner into the next related domain.

My personal journey began this way. I started out in the ministry as a personal evangelist, ministering one-on-one in witnessing situations. I then jumped domains when I figured out that I could preach revivals and ten people or more could receive Christ at one time. From there, I entered the pastorate, driven to understand why a revival preacher could harvest so many in one week and a pastor could work for years and see little fruit. I became very interested in growing my church. Next, I became a church planter, wanting to start healthy churches that saw fruit on a regular basis. This was all part of my ministry mindset.

I was jumping domains, learning the ropes in ministry. However, I still wasn't in the flow of the kingdom. I still wasn't seeing the bigger picture. Why? All of these domains related to business as usual. It's when I moved to the next level domains that had to do with kingdom work that things really started cooking (see figure 3).

The difference between the two levels is dramatic. A ministry focus is centered on what I can do with or without God. Learning the system and processes of how to run a church does not require a

Nation Building
Global Missions
Community Transformation
Church Multiplication (GlocalNet)
Church Mothering (NorthWood)

Planting a Church
Church Growth
Pastoring
Evangelistic Meetings
Personal Evangelism

Figure 3

kingdom mindset. Kingdom focus requires something beyond your own ability. It's what only God can do, with or without me. Ministry focus is systems, personal ability, processes, goals, and action plans. However, a kingdom focus means instead of existing for ourselves as a conduit to receive resources and people, we begin to exist to give away to others. Instead of existing to be a viable church, we now exist to be "multipliable." Whereas before we existed to get bigger in and of ourselves, now we existed to multiply churches in our communities and engage the nations. One of the biggest lessons I began to realize is that I could do all the ministry stuff and still not have an understanding or even embrace the kingdom of God. But multiplication and movements will not happen apart from the kingdom of God.

Let me give another illustration of how domain jumping works. Recently, clusters of churches that we have helped start over the past several years have banded together for the purpose of planting more churches together. One pastor shared a burden he had for planting college churches in our area. I'm convinced the greatest opportunity for planting is on college campuses. (Did you know there are around 1,200 universities in America? I do. We get mail from each one at least every other day now that my teenage daughter is about to graduate from high school.)

By our second meeting, the pastor shared his plan for starting over a hundred college campus churches in the next twelve years. We began to think as a group about combing our churches for teenagers who are going to college. *Where is the largest group of them going? Can we send them there and equip them to start a church on that campus and impact that community?* Since most of us had started our own churches, our students were already familiar with church planting.

But then it became really exciting. When they graduate and other kids come into those churches, what if they became pools of church multiplication material? Students who went on to graduate and work for various major corporations would then move to communities across the United States and start churches!

But don't stop there. A *global* culture of young college grads and college students exists. I've encountered them all around the world. These churches have more opportunity to engage in nation building than perhaps any group on the face of the earth ever has! What if God is raising up passionate college students for something like this? Do you get the picture? It's local *community development* and *church multiplication* and it's globally reproducible through *nation building*.

Seven

WHAT WOULD IT LOOK LIKE FOR THE CHURCH TO TURN THE WORLD UPSIDE DOWN?

Community Development
integral involvement in the community culture and morality

Does God care about the taxes that the poor pay? God led one of our young mothers, who happens to be a very successful corporate CPA, to do tax preparation for free in an area where most people living there couldn't afford it. One of her first clients was a lady who came in holding her children with one hand and last year's return with the other. Last year, she paid the tax preparer $300 and received a small refund. This year, she paid nothing and was able to land a refund of over $6,000. Was God glorified? Do you think it had an impact on this lady?

What would God have a church do for a nine-year-old and a six-year-old whose mom died four years ago with breast cancer and dad died six months ago after a massive heart attack? Leave them with their grandmother and a house falling apart? A group came together from NorthWood to do an extreme makeover on the home. Each week, they take them meals, clean the house, and do other things to help them. As those children get older, what impact will that have on them?

If the church were absent from the community would anyone miss it except for its own members? (Robert Lewis)

A public school principal accepted Christ at NorthWood and became involved in community service. One day at a board meeting, she heard two school administrators having a conversation about how a church has partnered with an inner city school (they were talking about her church, NorthWood). They were shocked at how well a school and a church could partner to impact a community.

These are just three stories, but there are countless others. From building Habitat houses, to English as a second language courses, to carnivals, to building projects at public schools, to medical clinics, to support group ministries—it goes on and on. You are limited only by the creativity of the people you are serving.

We recently had a fall festival at an inner city school. Two agnostic teachers were openly making comments like, "I've been all over this place, watching and listening to these church people ... and this is a different kind of church. They're truly out here for the community and have a desire to just love people." This is the kind of impact we want to make.

WHAT IF A CHURCH TURNED THE WORLD UPSIDE DOWN?

Isn't it ironic that America is growing churches by the thousands each year without transforming communities at the same rate? We believe we are evangelizing people, yet not making a dent in the culture's predominant morality. It makes one wonder, *What are we really doing?* In contrast, entire communities during the period of the early church and the Great Awakening were shaken to their moral and cultural foundations.

If local churches viewed themselves as missionaries, both locally and internationally, imagine what could be done! In my home state, there are approximately 5,000 churches in my denomination alone.

What could God do with just 2,000 churches across the nation that really went for all or nothing? How can it be that Coke and Boeing can do what they've done in America and all over the world, while the church, armed with the power of the gospel, has such little impact from here to the far corners of the globe?

Acts 17:6 says, "These men [i.e., the disciples] who have turned the world upside down have come here also" (RSV). That's a fascinating verse and an intriguing idea. Paul and company were literally turning the world upside down. Not just in their generation, but for the next twenty-one centuries of human history. Christianity would not only change the eternal destiny and present condition of countless lives, but it would also be the primary contributor to the future world order. Faith and learning would soon impact science, philosophy, business, politics, government, education, and nearly every other field of study.

Considering the odds of success and their limited connectedness to cultural and religious power structures of the day, it is truly a miracle that those early believers accomplished what they did. Throughout history, many good ideas and philosophies have come from better known and much more educated people than the disciples. But guess what? None of them "stuck" better than this one. What was humanly impossible became divinely inspired.

If the church ever gets in a position of radical transformation with its members, the potential for local and global impact is a given.

The same call to take the message and life of Christ to the world and demonstrate a new way of living that brings hope to lost humanity still exists. Yet, except for a new Christian or the hubris of the young, few people legitimately believe that they can transform a community, much less a nation. However, if we understand what it means to be a kingdom church and live in that context, we realize this is the very function of the church.

The church is not doing what it has been called to do until and unless it turns the world upside down.

A church that learns to church the area and influence the community cannot merely be a huddle or a gathering place to say kind things to one another. It will be an entity that is alive and powerfully spreading out in all directions.

For example, the church in China is turning communities upside down. There are reports now of Chinese going to other countries and people groups to make the message known. A recent report claimed Mongolian Christians (something that didn't exist a few decades ago) have now grown to over four hundred churches strong. Genghis Khan conquered nations all the way to Afghanistan! These modern day spiritual warriors have taken on the mandate of spreading the gospel with similar speed.

If the gospel were to spread at that clip in every community in the United States, what would it look like? One thing for sure, it wouldn't look like anything we've seen in the Western church to date. While we are building gymnasiums and coffee bars, fighting for the church's place in society's culture wars, others are spreading the gospel like wildfire and having an impact on how people are living.

ESSENTIALS FOR IMPACT

I believe five core elements are key descriptors of a church that will turn communities and eventually the world upside down. These things cannot be programmed; they are as organic and core to church identity as they are in China and other places in the world where the gospel is touching entire communities. We will look at a couple of them here in Community Development and the rest in the next chapter.

1. A church that turned the world upside down would look mystical.

2. A church that turned the world upside down would look glocal.

3. A church that turned the world upside down would be multiplying.

4. A church that turned the world upside down would be collaborative.

5. A church that turned the world upside down would be filled with ecclektricity.

A Church That Turned the World Upside Down Would Look Mystical

When I say "mystical," I mean experiencing God won't just be a course in a Sunday school class, it will be a lifestyle. Things will happen that you never would have dreamed of, planned for, or expected. The church today is paralyzed by one small word: wait. It calls for prayer meetings when it needs to take action. We see God moving around us daily everywhere we are, everywhere we go; the needs, the opportunities are there. We need desperately some Isaiahs that will say, "Here am I, Lord, send me."

In the Old Testament and New Testament, prayer seemed to mobilize the people and lead them to make a difference. For some strange reason today, instead of being a power source, prayer is the excuse for not doing anything, always "waiting on God" to do something, but it never happens. "Wait" always wants more information to delay pulling the trigger. The church of the future will be characterized by a different word altogether: risk. Powerful worship empowers us to go where no one wants to go and do things we ordinarily wouldn't do. An inner dimension of worship takes place within the lives of believers that moves them into a direction of incredible risk, courage, and action.

By mystical I also mean miraculous. God will bring opportunities and resources into your hands simultaneously and from the most unexpected places and people. I am always amazed at the resources God has put in my hands. The miraculous nature of God moving the world is undeniable (Matthew 9:35; Acts 5:12–16). However, it generally isn't the "charismatic style" and message of the Western church. It isn't a mystical prosperity focused on health and wealth. In fact, that's foreign to these people. Most of the stories circulating today in the East are about how God met a need in a divine way and touched a whole village.

A Church That Turned the World Upside Down Would Look Glocal

Most people think the Great Commission focuses on what is overseas; not so! It's both local and global—it's glocal. Len Sweet uses the word to describe culture. I use it to describe expansion and geography.

Glocal means operating in all dimensions.

The traditional idea has been to first win your backyard, then focus on your own country, then go overseas. A Transformed World operates in all dimensions at all times. The Great Commission was not sequential steps but dimensions we operate in simultaneously. It's not Jerusalem, then Judea, then Samaria, then the uttermost parts of the world. But Jerusalem, and Judea, and Samaria, and the uttermost parts of the world. Locally, we do all we can as a church to reach the lost. It also means we acknowledge our style alone will not reach them all, so we start other churches to hit the other segments of the community. We also operate nationally in church planting and work overseas by adopting an Unreached People Group. We operate simultaneously in all the dimensions. At no other time in history has this been easier to do. Remember, it is doable!

Glocal also means both showing the love of Christ and sharing the love of Christ. It may mean doing a medical clinic in Laos and building a Habitat for Humanity House in your town. It may mean door-to-door evangelism or it may mean Meals on Wheels. It's showing and sharing the love of God wherever you can.

A word of caution. Not everyone is going to operate in all dimensions, nor should they. However, every church should mobilize its people so that every member is operating in one of those dimensions—locally or globally. The people who get upset about all the overseas "missions" going on generally aren't involved in that dimension at all! They talk about "not neglecting our own fields," but they aren't building the Habitat houses, much less being intentionally evangelistic with their neighbors. A church will never balance what it does stateside and what it does locally to some people's satisfaction. The only answer is to stay on your face before God and then respond to what he puts in front of you. It then becomes less of a balancing act and more of a natural response to what God does.

Don't squabble about which dimension is the most important; they're all important. However, the more people that a church involves overseas, the more local impact in terms of giving and service results. Why? Those involved globally will come back changed, looking for a way to influence their world locally. In other words, the global must define the local or we will never get there, as Carol Davis once told me. I never understood that until I began to work globally. I thought they were two different things. They aren't. When we stretch way out, what is closest to us is forever changed.

WHEN LOCAL AND GLOBAL MERGE

Occasionally, the two dimensions merge where local and global become the same. When that happens, it's usually supernatural and always powerful. One summer after returning from an extended time in Asia, I discovered two families were involved in a local exchange-student program and expecting two students to live with them for the next year. The only problem was that they were from the very area we were working in—a "closed" country. It was a sensitive area and we'd heard many stories and even knew of some friends who had faced difficulties there for being Christians. To make matters worse, we soon discovered the prospective students were from families who happened to be high government officials. One student's father was almost as high up as one could go!

I was concerned because we talked about that particular area from the pulpit frequently to promote it among our people. Were these families willing to leave the church for a year in order not to threaten what God was doing? Nope, they weren't! They felt as if God had called them to do this. So we came up with all these rules and said we'd experiment with it, but if it didn't work, they'd have to visit another church. Some Sundays, when we had a special emphasis on that part of the world, these two families planned to leave on vacation with their exchange students! We even took down a lot of the art from that part of the world in our church so it would not create too many questions.

"We Never Felt God Like This"

The students weren't required to go to church, but they did! The first Sunday in the States, they sat together on the front row sleeping from jet lag! I was carefully dancing around them, petrified I'd say the wrong thing and mess up things. One Sunday they announced to their host families that they wanted to meet me! I met them and spoke as briefly as possible. To my surprise, these guys then started going to all the youth functions! They went on every youth retreat and never missed worship.

One Sunday, however, things shifted and I'll never forget it. We were singing in worship and the Spirit was moving. I glanced over at the youth "section" to see several were raising their hands. When I looked closer, I recognized one of the students lost in worship was the student whose father was a high government official, and his friend was next to him doing much the same. Their hands were stretched to heaven with tears streaming down their faces. My first response was, "Oh God, what if these kids become believers?" That was also my second response, "Wouldn't that mess up our work?" Ultimately, I lost it. I fell on my knees and began to pray for them and their families.

Another Sunday after worship, they came up to me and said, "You know, we've gone to the temple all our lives, but we never felt

God like this. He is real." A few months later, one of the students said, "I told my father I wanted to be a Christian, and he told me I must think carefully and know what I am doing."

A Key Conversation

My heart skipped a beat, and I told him we should sit down and talk at length. As God would have it, someone on our staff from that country was interning at the time, so he and his wife joined my family and the student at our house for dinner. We spoke for hours about why we believed there was one God and why we believed Jesus was the way to God. We shed many tears.

Finally, the student asked me, "Have you been to my country?" I had always avoided similar inquiries before. Finally, I couldn't ignore it anymore, and I conceded I'd "passed through" it.

"I thought so," he said self-assuredly. "I wondered how you could know so much about my country and why there were others here from my country. Why didn't you tell me?"

I explained I had understood that people went to jail sometimes for being Christians in his country. "With your dad in the government and all, I didn't want to go to jail!" I said.

It was getting late in the evening, but before he left, I drew a circle on a piece of paper and used the salt and pepper shakers to illustrate my question. I picked up the salt and placed it inside the circle, "This is you with Christ." I then left the other shaker outside the circle: "And this is you without Christ. Where are you?"

He took the saltshaker and put it over halfway there. I asked him, "What is keeping you from getting all the way over?"

Perfectly matter of fact, he replied, "If I believe that, then I have condemned my family. I must go back home and spend my life telling them about God and how Jesus loves them."

He was getting it. It wasn't just his salvation (that incidentally would happen only a month later), it was the salvation of his family and country! If only Americans understood that connection. This is not Las Vegas. What happens here does *not* stay here.

MORE THAN ACTS OF KINDNESS

This is glocal community development. It's here, it's there. It's here and there. It's back and forth and all over the place. It's modern dance, not what we call the Texas Two-step! What often slows down the tempo is that Western churches think in terms of measurement units they can understand. We in the West equate building family life centers and church libraries with credibility in the community. Buildings relate to our infrastructure and give us significance. However, if these endeavors are merely giving our own members other opportunities to shelter themselves even more from the world and not affecting the community, what is the merit? Ray Bakke proposes that churches can actually flow out of ministry! Now that's novel.

There are two approaches to community development: Start the church, or impact the community first through believers. This is the power of Steve Sjogren's random acts of kindness. I'd probably encourage you to do more than just wash windshields. Look at long-term things that can affect the community.

Everything we do around the world, we also attempt to do it locally.

Once I was at a brainstorming meeting about "missions" at a significant university where I am an adjunct professor. I made the statement that we needed to be not "missions minded" but "missional."

Someone piped up with, "We're doing some mission trips."

I responded pointedly, "I'm not talking mission trips. I'm talking missional in core and in strategy. If you want to be mission-minded, give international students scholarships; otherwise they won't be able to go to school. If you want to be missional, then start a campus in that country and help those people."

That was the last I thought I'd hear about it until the president of the university called me into his office. He asked me if I'd be open to using my relationships with the two students from Asia to explore the possibility of beginning a university in that country. I agreed. I called the father of one of the students, who had come to dinner at my house that night, made the arrangements, and headed over.

Once I was in Asia, the authorities greeted me and treated me with great respect. They all knew I was a pastor. The student's father asked me why I had never told anyone I was a pastor. I explained to him that I was afraid of being put in jail. He said we could keep doing humanitarian work in his country and talk to individuals as they asked questions about God. He gave me his card and told me if I had any issues, just show someone the card and there would be no more problems.

Something in our spirits and hearts knit—this was a good man who was curious about God. I felt I was with someone somewhere between Agrippa and Cornelius. Since then, we keep in touch via email and have become friends. Not only did his child receive a scholarship to the university; he has opened doors for us if we wanted to open a school there, too. That's another book on how we are structuring it! But one dimension of it is that we are going to try to educate as many of their nationals here as possible for them so that they can go back and teach in their home country. The students who come to live with our church families are in church every week!

The high schools are aware of the educational goals we have for these students, and many parents and teachers have opened their homes, too. What is happening here in our community has monumental potential for changing an entire country. It's glocal!

MISSIONS IN YOUR DNA

When churches think of themselves as "the missionary," it changes everything within the church. These are not churches that do missions; they are missions.[1] It's in their DNA. Churches must be willing to risk making mistakes because they are moving in a direction that the church hasn't moved in since the church first began! What a great place and exciting journey! We are not merely growing a church and building buildings. We are growing the church through local churches reaching their community and impacting the world simultaneously!

If missions is in your church's DNA, then you wind up with the wealth of resources of the people in your pews that can bring more impact than any single missionary couple can.

QUESTIONS TO THINK ABOUT AND TALK ABOUT

1. Why do you think people today view the church as "taking" from the community as opposed to giving and contributing to it?

2. What is the biggest need in your community that your church could address in order to make the biggest difference?

3. Has your church had a special service to recognize community leaders or won any special awards or recognitions for service? What might you do to increase this?

4. If you asked someone in your community who doesn't go to your church what your church is "known for," what would they say?

Eight

DO WE WANT TO BE THE BIGGEST CHURCH IN THE AREA, OR CHURCH THE AREA?

Church multiplication
transformed individuals who make up healthy churches
that, in turn, naturally grow and multiply

f I had to choose between starting ten churches that only grow to a hundred in a year or start one church that grows to a thousand in a year, I would prefer the ten churches with one hundred in attendance. Why? In time, many of those ten churches will surpass a thousand in attendance. If planting is in their DNA, in ten years they could have started fifty additional churches. What if they wound up only doing half of what we've done — that's 250 additional churches — and hopefully many of those will turn out to be church planting churches. However, if they surpass what we have pioneered and tripled it — which is usually the case — those ten churches could wind up with 1,500 church-planting churches, each adopting UPGs. And *local churches win the world, just as it was supposed to be!*

I have no interest in helping start a church — it's a waste of time and money. I have much interest in starting church-starting churches.

T-World involves a strategy of *church multiplication* that focuses on "missional" churches and movements that always outstrip individuals. T-World is not about starting churches. It's about fostering healthy kingdom-living in individuals who, in turn, make up healthy churches that naturally grow and multiply.

I am convinced that the key to the future is not church planting but church mothering. What's the difference? Churches do not plant churches, at least not in a methodological sense. Church planters plant churches. The job of the mother church is to come alongside people being called to plant and to assist them in whatever they need in order to be effective. The New Testament demonstrates only two intentional methods people used to spread the gospel. One was to share their faith one-on-one; the other was through planting churches, as Paul did, wherever they went. I believe people should be trained to plant churches throughout the world in various cultures, and mother churches should support the planters. Today, people are being called to become church planters like Paul. However, there are not enough church mothers partnering with them to get the job done.

WHAT IS THE CHURCH AND WHO IS THE PASTOR?

The missing ingredient of global evangelization is the local church. She's been raped and pillaged for all people could get from her. However, she's never been viewed as the primary arm of a movement, yet she is first and foremost. According to Scripture, it is the body of Christ proclaiming the message of Christ to help people grow in Christ. Therefore, the local church can be thought of more as a base from which spiritual military operations are designed, planned, and carried out. The church really is the sending structure, not just of a few but of all.

When we learn to mobilize local churches to move out to the ends of the earth, the Great Commission will become the Great Completion. I believe the hope of the Western church is tied to her ability to reconnect with her original call to advance into global evangelization. Jesus said in Matthew 11:12, "From the days of John the Baptist until now, the kingdom of heaven has been forcefully advancing, and forceful men lay hold of it."

If a church were a base, then the pastor would look less like a chaplain or preacher and more like a soldier mobilizing the troops for massive advances. I didn't realize my new role until a few years after we got into that mode of operation. In fact, when I once asked a panel of my advisors, "Do you think of me more as a preacher or as a pastor?" the response was intriguing.

One of the men quickly said, "Neither." That concerned me, since we were evaluating my role and the church. Fortunately, he swiftly followed that statement with another: "Bob, you're a soldier, and you're turning this church into an army!"

He was right. I had evolved into a new paradigm for the role of a senior pastor. In the T-World model, the role of the pastor undergoes specific shifts—from chaplain/preacher to soldier/diplomat. From a stateside motivator to the in-the-field model of how it's to be done. The pastor becomes a mobilizer, a researcher, a strategist, and a networker.

CHURCH PLANTING STRATEGY

If the church is both the body of Christ and the primary vehicle for globally expanding the kingdom, church planting is the primary strategy whereby we accomplish this goal. In the last twenty years, church planting movements have affected tribes and some cultures, and perhaps even a country or two. However, what if a global Church Planting Movement (CPM) connected the entire body of Christ worldwide? I will live and die for a vision like that. I have a twofold personal goal to reach by the time I am sixty years old:

- to start one church for every UPG, either in the West or somewhere else in the world;
- to serve the UPGs to help them bring about their own CPM that will move out to other parts of world.

I want to be a part of one of the world's first global Church Planting Movements (CPM).

It's Not Just about Your Church

One of the best ways to launch your strategy for church planting is to start a church nearby to remind you it isn't all about your campus. It's best to get over your own feelings of competitiveness between churches right away. When we first began planting churches, we knew we were going to have to look beyond what we could fit into our buildings and on our land. We helped a young man named Sam Carmack as he started Bear Valley Community Church. Later, another young man, Doug Walker, started Fellowship of the Parks. Today, we have planted close to eighty churches throughout the United States, seven of them in our area.

A gifted pastor who has networked with GlocalNet has a seven-year-old church where already close to 3,000 attend. On Easter Sunday, he called me recently and said, "Bob, you're not going to believe this! In our new church plants, one had over 400 and another had over 500!" He was more excited about the attendance at his new church plants than he was the 5,500 at his location! I've been there! I get excited when I drive past other churches that we've helped plant all over the United States and know we had some part in it.

Some people have questions. Did we ever fail to plant a successful church? Do we work only within our denomination? Yes, we've experienced failure. We started another church in the area but it didn't survive. Yes, we worked outside our denomination too. We also helped three other churches outside our denomination that were in need of some mentoring in their early phases. However, if "missions" is in your church's DNA, you will keep going despite failure. You will reach your own community because those whom you face everyday will be your burden.

In that sense, the church will be rightfully concerned about growth and health. However, many pastors will tell you they've been called to reach their community, only sadly it stops at their acreage. If they could only see that they've been called to "church" the entire area! This will mean moving in the next dimension of T-World and starting multiple churches and multiple forms of churches around you to reach different people groups in any given community.

It could be house churches, cowboy churches, postmodern churches, contemporary churches, boomer churches, seeker churches. But it doesn't stop in the community alone. Next, it's your state and then your nation. But it doesn't stop there either. Focus on a UPG and see the world. Now, as never before in the history of humanity, it's time for a "kingdom church" to engage the world.

DANGER IN COPYING A MODEL

It's time for us to learn to think again. There was a time when the pastor was the sharpest person in the community. Not anymore. If anything, we celebrate ignorance. I remember once asking a friend of mine for a reference regarding a potential pastor and he told me, "Bob, he's ignorance on fire!" And he was. It's time for us to think and engage our minds like never before.

Church planting is one of the most interconnected strategies a church can implement. We can never keep it in a single dimension; it always spills over into the next. As a result, we also work with house churches in closed countries throughout the globe. We plant large churches, small churches, and medium-sized churches. We plant cowboy churches, denominational churches, seeker churches, postmodern churches, ethnic churches — any kind of church!

The common bond of church-planting churches is the genetic makeup, the DNA, that makes all of them multiplying churches.

This multifaceted operation did not happen because we studied church planting and developed a strategy with systems and goals. Nor did we look for a model we could "copy" and implement here. Models are not for us to copy, but to learn from and adapt to our own unique setting. Too often we skip over what would be healthy for our church in favor of what's popular and flashy in another church. (How else could our churches be considered "healthy" despite the fact that most are infertile in terms of reproducing itself in another church?) A strategy should never be adopted because it worked for someone else. To mimic means not only that you will copy the good, but often unintentionally the bad as well. That's dangerous.

To mimic takes absolutely no creativity.

Three Steps Forward ... Two Steps Back

Most of what we know about church planting has been born out of a struggle that took us three steps forward and two steps back. That's why strategies must fit in with an evolving understanding of all that God has called you to do and made you into so that you can fulfill his purpose and the vision you see for the future. The question really is not, "Which model am I going to follow?" but "Which community do I live in and how do they think?" That's the difference between mimicking a model and designing a church.

My goal is not that churches would follow the T-World model to the last detail, but that they would follow its design and the basic principles as it relates to their unique setting. Churches will be multiple and varied. There will be many expressions because never has our culture been more diverse and (sadly) segmented than it is today. Just as no two people are identical, neither are churches. Each community has its own history, demographics, psychographics, economics, and stories.

Keep in mind that strategies for developing a church were never intended to last forever. A pitfall of strategy is that it becomes fixed and unchangeable. I like what seminary professor Roy Fish says, "Marry yourself to one method in a single generation, and you'll be a widow in the next."[1] He's right. The entire premise of this book is that things change, and only an understanding of design based on who you are and what God has called you to do will work for churches in the present and future. Change is happening too fast, and God is always up to something new. Only those who flow with him and the culture will stay alive and relevant. Church planting is not a program we can package; it is a natural, organic outflow. For some this is scary, but once one takes the first step, there will be no going back.

KEY DESCRIPTORS OF CHURCH MULTIPLICATION

In the previous chapter, we introduced five core elements or key descriptors of a glocal church that will turn communities and also the world upside down. We examined the *mystical* and *glocal* elements as they relate to Community Development. Now let's examine the remaining three core elements as they relate to Church Multiplication.

A Church That Turned the World Upside Down Would Be Multiplying

The world's first global church planting movement would move beyond a tribe, people group, or single nation to encompass all nations and all peoples. On Saturday nights, I often think about how Asians, Australians, and other people in different parts of the world are already beginning their worship services. When I stand to preach on Sunday mornings, I'm intrigued by the fact that most of the world has already worshiped, and we in the West are the last to bring it on home. There is no building large enough to hold all of the kingdom of God. It's that huge.

In the early days of my ministry, I defined how the kingdom of God was growing by what was happening in my church and my tribe. However, we must not allow our vision of the kingdom to be limited by what we can see. It's not that I didn't respect the other tribes; I just was not a part of them and didn't know them very well. The more I'm involved in starting churches, working overseas, and networking with the rest of the body of Christ, the more I see how powerful and extensive the kingdom really is.

Social scientists and historians describe hinge points in history and technology where one discipline begins to explode, changing the future exponentially. Today, every academic discipline and area of technology is exploding—internet communication, medicine, energy, transportation, computers, digital media, and so on. Together, we *can* complete the Great Commission if we do it exponentially. The church is large enough. The Holy Spirit is powerful enough. But our dreams are not big enough. Many who talk about church growth paint a picture of buying large parcels of land and building auditoriums with thousands of seats. That's a great dream. But God's dreams are much greater. God sees millions stretched across his canvas, not thousands.

Exponential growth is amazing. At first, our goal was to plant three churches in five years. Today, we've planted eighty. We started with one church-planting intern each year. Today, we have eighteen interns who will help us plant ten church-planting churches this year. If we invest all our resources to help plant a church that will be an end in itself, we've wasted time and money. However, if we focus on starting only churches that are going to start other churches, then we multiply our efforts dramatically.

For this reason, we have certain requirements of our planters. I don't look for church planters. I look for those who can train, equip, and deploy church planters. In a multiplying mindset, we would value the planter who plants a single church that, in turn, plants ten more churches in ten years more than we would value a single church that grew to ten thousand in ten years. You know a church is multiplying when it has as many or more "granddaughter" churches than it has "daughter" churches.

We will grow by over 3,600 people at our church this year, but they won't all be in our NorthWood campus sanctuary. Will our church grow locally? Yes! Will it be a church of several thousand one day? Sooner than later. How can that be? Exponential multiplication.

There is nothing greater you can do for the church of tomorrow than to plant her churches today!

However, if we went the traditional route of focusing only on ourselves, we might plateau at 10,000 or 15,000, or 20,000 on our membership rolls. Reverse engineering isn't possible at that point to inject the missional DNA back into the church if it wasn't there from the start. Churches caught in the debate between planting churches or growing their own local church lose on both counts. The answer? Do both. Not doing one is not an excuse for not doing the other. Multiplying churches grants us the potential to see the world's first global church planting movement emerge this century, if not within the first two decades.

A Church That Turned the World Upside Down Would Be Collaborative

Obviously turning the world upside down starts first with mobilizing its own members as we have already studied, but it also means going beyond that to networking and working with all believers who want to see the kingdom expand.

Collaboration moves beyond the individual. No one single church is going to win the world, but glocal kingdom churches are winning the world as they collaborate their efforts. Collaboration as part of the universal body of Christ requires everyone of us. We will stand together or die alone. If we are one body, as Paul describes in his first letter to the Corinthians, we are in need of emergency surgery to stop the bleeding, sew it up, and make a full recovery! If we allow Christ to heal our wounds and put us back together again, we will be healthy. However, imagine if we attempt this spiritual surgery on the Church alone—we may end up with something more like a Frankenstein!

One of the most frequently used words in the entire Bible is the word "together."

Together in Christ! "For where two or three *come together in my name*, there am I with them." (Matthew 18:20, italics added in all places)

Together in the Spirit! "When the day of Pentecost came, *they were all together* in one place." (Acts 2:1)

Together in the church! "Every day they continued to *meet together* in the temple courts. They broke bread in their homes and *ate together with glad and sincere hearts*." (Acts 2:46)

Together in service! "In him the whole building is *joined together* and rises to become a holy temple in the Lord. *And in him you too are being built together* to become a dwelling in which God lives by his Spirit." (Ephesians 2:21–22)

Together in power! "And I pray that you, being rooted and established in love, *may have power, together* with all the saints...." (Ephesians 3:17–18)

Together in the clouds! "After that, we who are still alive and are left will *be caught up together with them in the clouds* to meet the Lord in the air." (1 Thessalonians 4:17)

Scripture assures us, both in the local church and the global church, that unity is not optional. Unlike past church movements initiated by a gifted pastor or revivalist, I see the next movement eclipsing a single individual. My dream is to be a part of one of the world's first global church-planting movements. My dream is that it would merit the attention of historians who reflect back on what takes place and conclude, "It was not because of any one of them, but because of all of them." Collaboration excels what a single church can do or what a single individual can do. Individuality cannot take us where we need to go. No one exists today or will emerge in the future with all of the pieces to the puzzle.

*Great dreams don't just require a great
person—but great people.*

Collaboration also means each individual has a role. When we learn to work together, we will find we must rely on one another for those roles. Don't worry about the percentage of population yet to hear about and accept Christ. If you are faithful to your particular contribution to the whole, you will be faithful to the overall cause. Don't worry about how accessible the country is that God is putting on your heart to reach and to touch. Accessibility doesn't always mean people will follow Christ. For example, Thailand is open to evangelism, yet the church is generally weak. However, it's illegal to evangelize in China, and the church is unstoppable.

Paul saw himself as a fellow laborer with others. The church that gets it done will always have others involved in collaborative efforts.

A Church That Turned the World Upside Down Would Be Filled with Ecclektricity

I push our church planters to learn from every model, but not to mimic any model. The kingdom of God is so huge; it will not be limited to a single form or style but to many kinds. The *ecclesia* is the church that moves in the culture; it's the vehicle for the kingdom of God. However, what God does is also creative and "eclectic"—it's different for each culture and for each time in history. I tell church planters all the time, "If you leave this place and try to 'do North-Wood' somewhere, we've failed you. Instead, know yourself, the people, and God's Word and design it to who you are." Ecclektricity is celebrating the diversity in the body of Christ and recognizing the value that it brings.

In other words, we can celebrate all of the different forms and styles instead of being suspicious. Ecclektric churches will engage and celebrate the diversities by inclusion, not exclusion (Ephesians

3:6–11). As we affirm one another, a certain amount of energy results like a charge of electricity.

In ecclektric churches:

- every ethnic race matters — Vietnamese, Hispanic, Chinese, Anglo — because every race matters to God
- every generation matters — builders, boomers, busters, millennials — because every generation matters to God
- every caste matters — rich, poor, and in between — because every caste matters to God
- every nation matters — Iraq, Iran, North Korea, Sudan, Libya, even those unrecognized nations such as the Kurds and Palestinians — because every nation matters to God
- every tribe matters — Cherokee, Shashonee, Pygmy, Aboriginal — because every tribe matters to God
- every culture matters — premoderns, moderns, postmoderns, preconvergents — because every culture matters to God

Those who define church only by their context are not just narrow-minded (some would say dense), but they are also in for the ultimate great awakening when they arrive in heaven!

I have often heard those in my tribe claim, "Our strength is in our diversity." However, it was always a bunch of white guys saying that! They all used the same methods and, as a result, their churches were virtually identical. One could visit a church in Dallas, Los Angeles, or Washington, D.C., and see no visible difference. Diversity is more than having a Hispanic church and a few African Americans on your campus every week. As a whole, my tribe was driven by one style, one format, and one race.

God's Kingdom Is Bigger

One day I was driving with our gifted associate pastor, Phuc "Frank" Dang, on my way to teach a church-planting class at seminary. He started talking about what it might look like if he started a church. He envisioned a second-generation church for Asians, which allows for an easy mix of Chinese, Vietnamese, Laotian, Korean, and so on. As he debated the pros and cons, I challenged him to look beyond the Vietnamese. "God's kingdom is bigger than any race or nation," I prodded.

I began to challenge him further, "Phuc, you are a gift and blessing to the whole body of Christ, not just Vietnamese. Dude, I love you because you are Phuc, not because you are Vietnamese."

Multiplying churches that practice ecclektricity move from a single race to leadership within the mainstream. If I were going to plant another church, I think I'd design a multiethnic church, a type of church I believe will be huge in the future. Furthermore, I would build a multiethnicity that extended equally among the staff as it would its members. As NorthWood has learned more about kingdom expansion, we've moved from hiring all Anglo interns and planting all Anglo, suburban churches to planting churches of different races and different places.

The question is, *What does it really mean to be inclusive?* As a whole, the Anglo church respects and values the different races. We also want to help them in any way we can (as long as it doesn't hurt us or infringe on what we do). But I do believe we have ignored them. We see them as less than ourselves; otherwise, white guys would not primarily fill our ministry meetings. I grieve that I myself was so "white" in my perspective for so many years.

Recently in my seminary class, I began to share what God was doing in the world through church multiplication. I happened to know two of the international students sitting in the class, as they are interns at our church. Unbeknownst to them and without mentioning names, I told their stories. People were visibly moved to hear of the huge price two young men had paid for the sake of the gospel. I then casually said, "Oh, by the way, they're also your classmates." The rest of the class was stunned! How could someone that exceptional be among them without their having any idea. They had never been rude to these two men; most of them just failed to "see" them.

My Pastor Is Asian—He Just Has White Skin

My children, my wife, and I were walking in the mall a few months ago. I heard my son and daughter whispering together—it sounded as if they were counting: "One, two, three …" Then they would both smile as if they shared a secret joke. After an hour of this, I finally asked them, "What are you doing?"

Ben spoke up, "We're playing the Asian Game, Dad."

"What's that?" I asked.

"When we see an Asian, we start counting until you notice him and try talking to him!"

Busted! It's true—I've come to love all kinds of races, especially Asians, but this has only happened in the past few years. I am convinced that had we not initially traveled overseas, we wouldn't feel that way toward Asians. However, once we began to interact with them overseas, all of a sudden we started seeing them here as if for the first time. We saw them, not because they had just started coming to America, but because we were seeing them for the first time here!

One Wednesday night one of our interns, who happens to be Asian, inadvertently paid my church the ultimate compliment when he said, "When I came here, I thought I was going to intern at a white church and have a white teacher to help me. But, I feel these people *are* Asian. My pastor *is* Asian, he just has white skin."

No One Is Exempt

I'll never forget the man who came into my office one day saying he wanted to start a church for Hispanics. To emphasize his point, he led me to my window, pointed to the houses and yards around our campus, and said, "The maids, the landscapers, even the road crews maintaining our streets are all from Mexico." I was afraid of what I thought he was going to say next.

He wasn't afraid to say it. "I want to start a church for illegal aliens," he announced, tapping on the windowsill.

My first inclination was to sheepishly respond, "That's against the law, isn't it?"

Then it hit me: What have we been doing in other parts of the world where it's illegal? Just because they are not citizens, does that make them ineligible for the gospel? God convicted me at that moment how blind I have been to those around us and what they need.

Ecclektricity thunderbolts beyond races and culture, across styles of worship, too. I experience God in our worship at NorthWood, but I have also experienced him in worship in a Presbyterian church with a Catholic priest, Henri Nouwen. How tragic that we relate the form of worship to our ability to communicate with God more than carrying the substance from service to service. High church, low church, house church, open church, underground church, charismatic church, traditional church, contemporary church — God is in all forms. But its only function — if that church is alive — is to allow God's kingdom to flow into people's lives.

Those obsessed with style just don't get it. Styles are not the goal, only conduits — and only for a period in time. I used to think styles were important until I discovered that it wasn't a style, a format, a preacher, or even a style of preaching. Jesus became my focus and obsession.

The good news is that most new churches come from established churches that are over ten years old. That means any established church can get involved in church multiplication. The bad news, however, is that most of those established churches have never started a church, and it will be difficult for both the established and the new church. The answer? It's twofold. We must simultaneously recalibrate established churches to plant on a regular basis while new churches are infused with a whole new DNA from day one so that they will be church-planting churches.

STARTING CHURCHES VERSUS MULTIPLYING KINGDOM COMMUNITIES

No church will impact the world without growing where it is. No church that ignores the world and church planting is a biblical church. It's both/and. When I hear people say they are going to "grow here first (meaning their local campus) and then we'll grow a church," I know they don't get it. Equally ignorant is the statement, "We're going to start churches instead of focusing on our church." It's not either/or; it's both/and.

You see, it's not about church planting. It's about the larger kingdom. Let the kingdom define the church, and not the church the kingdom. What does that mean? It means the following:

- At their very best, local churches should be expressions of God's kingdom, alive and active.

- Never start a church for a community or for a target group. Start a church for the world, based out of a community with a specific target group.

- Think along the lines of eternity, not quick fixes for growing areas. Rick Warren taught me that the pastor who is at a single church for life makes radically different decisions from the one who is there for a season.

- Likewise, a church that is birthed out of a passion for the kingdom and for God to be glorified looks very different from a church that started because of "all those people moving into the area."

- When the focus is on kingdom communities and not just church plants, there is no room for competition among churches. If I focus on growing the kingdom, other churches and plants are not my competitors; they are my partners.

- It's about sharing resources outside your church, not just hoarding them for inside your church. Remember, what's good for your church may not be best for the kingdom. Generosity must extend beyond our members to other churches and other communities, locally and around the nation and world.

- Celebrate the kingdom. Tell the stories of what God is doing in the lives of those whom God has called out of your church to start other churches.

It's not just church planting that makes for a transformed world. Churches must engage the world. But how does a church do that?

QUESTIONS TO THINK ABOUT AND TALK ABOUT

1. What is the ethnic, economic, and demographic makeup of your community?

2. At best, how many kinds of people can your church relate to here? What kinds of people live here that your church can't naturally connect with?

3. What would be the first church we should plant if we wanted to impact our community?

4. When was your church started? When did you start your first church? When could you start your next church?

Nine

WHAT DO YOU GET WHEN A CHURCH COMBINES BILLY GRAHAM WITH MOTHER TERESA?

Nation building
leveraging natural infrastructures for maximum global impact

Many churches may drop some bucks and take a few trips, but in terms of intentionally sacrificing all for the sake of the world, I don't see it happening—at least, not yet.

When different denominations ask me to take some of their megachurch pastors on "vision trips" overseas, I've taken one or two (though my time is too tight to take an entire group). Their first question often is, "When do I get to preach?"

My response is, "Never. Welcome to missions in the twenty-first century."

We're not going there to preach, we're going there to serve. It's not about our preaching; it's about his kingdom. We're primarily there to sweep floors and find connections for our laypeople to use their gifts and contacts with corporations.

TRANSFORMED LIVES ON DISPLAY

Nation building in T-World is the story of Acts all over again, using business, trade, transportation, and other natural infrastructures as a means to see the world changed. It is the story of average church members touching nations through their jobs and through transformed lives on display. Ask Westerners who is the best Christian they know, and they'll tell you Billy Graham. Ask non-Westerners, and they'll say Mother Teresa. T-World is a marriage between the two. It is serving and boldly proclaiming. It is loving for love's sake, whether they follow Christ or not, not using the gospel as some sort of religious bait. It is the unrestrained outward expression of the kingdom inside of us.

CHOOSING A NATION

NorthWood focuses on one spot in particular, but I'm all over the globe looking for where the churches we are planting in the United States can explore the next initiatives. Our own journey of choosing a nation to focus upon began with one encounter. In 1992, a local surgeon who had been an agnostic found God. A year later, he began serving on our missions task force at a time when we were beginning to start churches stateside and praying about a specific UPG to adopt. I had thought about China or East Europe or somewhere maybe in the Middle East. Instead, he suggested a country I'd never considered.

When I was a young man, my father had pastored near an Air Force base where many pilots trained for service in that country. My mom often invited the soldiers over on Sunday afternoons, where they taught my brother and me how to spit shine our shoes and told us war stories that scared us to death. When we'd hear that some of them left and weren't coming back, I resented the ones who took my heroes away from me.

That country was the last country I wanted our church to adopt.

But how would I admit to a new, enthusiastic Christian (who had fought there and been shot down three times over that country) that I didn't want to go there? I quickly inventoried my pastoral arsenal of spiritual excuses and offered, "Well, let's just pray about it." I learned in seminary that if you can't stop it, slow it by calling for prayer!

As God would have it, I received an invitation the next day from a major missions organization to visit that very country. They didn't know our discussions or what we were looking at doing. This was from God. So, rather begrudgingly but intrigued, I went.

Due to security issues, we could not fly to the main city as we intended. So we landed in another part of the country on an abandoned Air Force base I had seen pictures of in magazines and books. As we sat on the tarmac, sweating in the hot plane, I saw remnants from the war scattered all over the place. I thought to myself about how many body bags had lined this runway, waiting to be taken home to be buried. When they finally opened the plane door, I must admit I was prepared not to like anyone I would meet. By the end of our trip, I was still nervous, but I knew God still wanted me there. When I told the group I was with that I intended to fly on to the main city alone, they warned me of the danger. However, I felt compelled by something I didn't yet understand.

A Wild Taxi Ride

When I arrived in the city later that evening, I was the only person who spoke English, and I was without a translator. Above the din of the crowd and the roar of commotion, I somehow heard a familiar word, "Taxi!"

I headed toward the voice shouting to me. The taxi driver took my fare, and before I knew it, a dozen people had piled into the mini-van along for the ride. They were crammed together, top, bottom, and sides. It was wild! What should have been a fifteen-minute ride to my hotel took three hours since I had unwittingly financed the others' rides, too. The first person to greet me was an unfriendly police officer. He wasted no time wanting to know who I was, where I came from, and why I was there so late alone. Dissatisfied with my answers, he kept my passport and sent me to bed. I remember thinking, "I've blown it now. I'll never be heard from again and no one will know where to find me."

Falling in Love with a City

The next morning, a man with a rickshaw-type bicycle was outside the hotel. He motioned for me to get on and I did. He effortlessly pedaled me all over the entire city that day, and I fell in love with it.

He asked me in his broken English, "Chris-tin?"

"Yes," I said. Immediately, he took us on a route so I could see every temple in the city!

The people, whom I had been told were cold and rude, were not at all. They were as warm as any East Texan I had ever known—I had only hoped they wouldn't be as mean! In fact, when my driver and I would get out, he insisted on holding my hand! At first, I didn't like that and pulled away. (I'm from East Texas and no men I knew did that.) However, the only people who didn't smile were the soldiers. Whenever they'd pass us, he could hold my hand all he wanted!

In a single day, God captured my heart for an entire nation. When I arrived home, I relayed to our missions task force what I had experienced, and we deemed this country our UPG to focus on for the next several years. NorthWood accepted the personal call to missions—she had her field.

RISK IS INHERENT

I learned a big lesson from my experience of choosing a nation. It's time for the church to get busy and not pay someone else to do what it doesn't want to do. Risk has become the missing element of the American church. We think we have the option of deciding if we should go or not. We go out on a limb to incur debt, but little else. But history is the story of people who did what others thought was too insignificant, too dangerous, or too undesirable.

The captain of the Gerkas in Nepal (who was in charge of the king's palace and a personal aid of the king before he was murdered in Katmandu) is a friend of mine. He and I were talking one day about leadership. I asked him, "What is your goal as a captain?"

He thought about it for a moment before responding, "The goal of a leader of Gerkas is that he causes men to do what they would never want to do so that they would be inspired and do it with joy."

I told him, "You'd make a great church planter!"

He laughed and said, "But I am a Hindu!"

To which I smiled and said, "Well, we can fix that!"

That's our job as pastor/soldiers. We have no right to mark danger off our lists. Living out a T-World will cost you—financially, emotionally, even physically. The price could be someone's life. Secret police, war, violence—we run from these things. In the West, we've insulated ourselves from the danger and viewed it as an option. What if Paul and the early church had our mindset? There would be no church today. Fortunately, that wasn't Paul's approach and that isn't the way the world will be reached.

There are no closed nations, and there are no nations that won't accept our help—even in the name of Jesus. They just won't accept our Western version of entertainment superstar preachers who refuse to humble themselves and go in as servants to these nations despite the dangers.

I'm convinced that when we live the gospel as radically as it was lived in Acts, it will be just as dangerous.

Risk is inherent, but it can also be invigorating when we realize our faith is there to uphold us when it becomes difficult. We have to realize that when we accepted Christ, we gave him our life. In essence, we are already dead—no one can take our life from us. As a pastor, I've watched people die slowly with disease and cancer in tremendous pain at times. There are worse ways to go than a quick bullet or sharp blade. We are all going to have to die someday, somehow. Why not let your exit be your finest moment? Don't try to lose your life; just don't fear it when it comes. If you do fear, just breathe deeply and know you are not alone.

Risk must be measured, of course, with wisdom. Risk can kill you—and it can be good or bad, wise or foolish risk.

CHOOSING YOUR OWN UPG

I wish I would have understood some of what I am sharing with you before we began our own journey. Thankfully, God's grace is sufficient to help you even when you are ignorant. There are several ways to discover a UPG, city, or unreached corner of the world.

Look. See if there are large populations in your area from other countries in the world. Are they refugees? That will enable you to know humanitarian strategies. Do they comprise the work force? That will enable you to use business and technology as strategies.

Study. Study the different parts of the world and the various UPGs and see which one you fit with the best. There are many agencies and groups from Adopt-A-People Clearing House to the International Mission Board in Richmond, Virginia, that will help you discover what UPGs have not been reached. What strengths do you bring to that particular country's needs? The only problem is, most organizations aren't ready for churches like this and often don't know what to do with them. Make sure they understand your church wants to do far more than just fund their projects, having eternal prayer walks and taking a trip. Your church wants to go deep within the culture so that your own laypeople can begin easing into the culture.

Learn. Learn to sincerely love the people and the country you are working with and in, but also know that they are to be mobilized to the ends of the earth instead of staying home.

Focus. Keep the end in mind; never lose focus there. I tell the people in and from the country that we work in that our goal is not just the evangelization of that country but of the world. I also tell them that if they go back to their country, for them that isn't missions; it's going home. They must focus on a unique place in the world and begin to tackle it.

Choose. I've seen people take years to decide whom they are going to reach. If you can't decide, then just focus on one and move forward. Why do we make it so hard? If you sincerely can't decide, come alongside others who are already working somewhere and partner with them for a while. Learn from this mentoring relationship and then perhaps head to the group nearest your mentors.

Pray. Above all, pray. God will lead.

Get ready for a lot of fog on the whole UPG issue. Some people say there are 4,000 UPGs, some say only 2,000 UPGs. Some even claim only 200 UPGs are left unreached. You need to understand their definition of UPG and what "reached" means. For some organizations, if you just adopt a UPG, whether it has a church-planting movement or not, it is considered "reached." Certainly, most of them are in the 10/40 window. The last remaining groups are most heavily concentrated from India on into the Middle East. However, there are UPGs on every continent.

FRONT DOOR EVANGELISM

Since we began focusing on this particular UPG, several hundred people have gone from our church in many different areas of humanitarian work in this country, sharing our faith as people ask. And oddly enough, they always ask! If the church is going to be an effective missionary involved in nation building, she may look more like Mother Teresa today than William Carey. In other words, we will not look like the typical twentieth-century missionary when we're in action.

We are not "using" humanitarian aide just to get to the "real work" of the gospel. Our service is the real work.

Pure Motives for Evangelism

We must love people and serve them regardless if they "say the prayer." If we genuinely love people as God's creation, then many of them will become believers. However, if our primary motivation of humanitarian aide is only to "convert" them and not to practice Christ's love in feeding the thousands and healing the sick (even knowing, as Jesus himself did, that some would not follow), then that negatively influences what we proclaim. What then is the motivation of our evangelism? What does that say about our sincere love of others?

I serve not as a "bait" but because it is the nature of Christ in me. Who would help a hurting person on the side of the road and then demand, "Accept Jesus because I helped you." Absurd! The kingdom is not just about proclamation to the nations; it's about inauguration. It's about healing; it's about helping—digging wells, feeding the hungry, building shelters, teaching farming, opening up small microbusinesses; all of these and a thousand other things are ways we emphasize God's love for the nations. We communicate that we're here for the long haul and we care. That's how we earn credibility.

Earning Credibility Overseas

A few years ago, because of some unusual circumstances, I met with some government officials in a war-torn country to see how we could serve their physical needs. They needed help with hospitals, universities, and humanitarian aide—something our laypeople work with every day. I told them right away that I was a Christian and made it clear I wouldn't force God down their throats. However, I also told them that if I shared my faith or if others had conversations with people one-on-one about God, I didn't want to have to worry about anyone being arrested. Those with whom I would be networking back in America to provide help wouldn't want to be "secret" Christians. Do you know what their response was? The highest official thanked me for being honest and open with him. Then he said, "You are welcome here."

That's what I mean about going through the front door. We are not working in these other countries to confront or criticize their culture. We are not trying to impose American culture (and certainly not American Christianity) on them. In fact, we are creating an entirely new culture—the culture of the kingdom. We are looking for opportunities to touch, relate to, and serve the existing culture in order to, over time, convey what the kingdom culture is like.

MOBILIZING NATIONALS

If the church is going to be an effective missionary involved in nation building, she must mobilize laity and nationals as well. Why? The day of the white man going and starting churches among nationals is over. For years, I would pray with the best intentions, "O God, reach this nation and cause them to come to faith in you." I no longer pray that kind of prayer. Instead, I pray, "God, from this nation, raise up the greatest pastors, missionaries, teachers, and leaders for your kingdom that the world has yet seen. From this nation, raise up believers who will take the world by storm for your kingdom." Jesus himself encouraged us to pray along these lines: "Then he said to his disciples, 'The harvest is plentiful but the workers are few. Ask the Lord of the harvest, therefore, to send out workers into his harvest field'" (Matthew 9:37–38).

This shift toward grafting more nationals into missions has been gradually taking place over the years. Still, to a large degree, the Westerner has often initiated the movement only to encounter difficulty in disengaging. Furthermore, there is always the tension of Western Christian culture versus indigenous Christian culture. Nationals are more readily open to receiving the gospel. This trend is going to speed up more and more. As the developing world becomes more effective in reaching their own cultures and educated in their ability to share their stories, the primary role of the Westerner will continue to diminish. For too long, Christian workers have felt they had to help the nationals; they were too weak and uneducated. Not anymore.

Using Nationals as Missionaries

Kingdom extension expands exponentially when nationals are the ones who are driving the work. The goal is not the "work" or the "job" that the missionary does, but the spread of the gospel. God is calling more than just the white culture to be the missionaries. It's tragic that we go over to help people hear about Christ but develop evangelistic strategies without any national input. Nationals need more than input—they need to be the designers of the strategies.

Nationals in any culture reach nationals better than anyone else does.

Though you may be at risk, the nationals who wish to help extend the kingdom take the greater risk. Most of the time, their officials will just put an American on a jet and send him or her out. They put their own people in prison and won't let them out. If they're willing to risk so much, we cannot passively observe their suffering and persecution.

Paul says in 1 Corinthians that when one part of the body suffers, the whole body does. Tragically, we are just putting the trials of our own spiritual family members out of our minds. We wonder if we get too close to them, the same will happen to us. I believe it will.

I believe people today, especially young people, will face some of the hardest challenges and difficulties of anyone, anywhere. Does God love them less and therefore they have to suffer? Or does God love us more and doesn't make us have to go through what they go through? Neither. We all face what we must to extend the kingdom of God.

One of the most gifted, brilliant young men I've ever met in my life was a mountain guide in the Himalayas named Kumar (who also happened to be a church planter). As the Anglos sat in a meeting room discussing how to best reach his country, he sat at the end of the table. He should have been at the front of the class leading the session. I wonder how much longer it will be before the missionary force of mission agencies moves from being primarily white Westerners to becoming racially diverse nationals living in their own countries as it is in China.

Equipping nationals who are less expensive, just as smart, and already know the language and culture just makes sense. Their effectiveness will always outstrip a Westerner. That isn't an insult to us as much as it exposes the fact that we aren't being smart about how we strategize.

Tradition dies hard; it is often more valuable to most mission institutions than the spread of the kingdom.

BUILDING FOR THE FUTURE

Phuc Dang, our associate pastor from Asia, is one of God's gifts not just to his ethnicity but also to the entire body of Christ. He has a burden for his people and his country. He will and he must work there—but he will never stop there.

He came to the United States at the age of nineteen after living in a bamboo hut as a child while his father was in a reeducation camp. His dad, who had been a doctor in Asia, escaped to America on a boat and immediately began to work and save money painting houses. His goal was to earn enough money so that he could bring his wife and other children over to the States. Phuc couldn't speak any English when he arrived, but he took a college entrance exam and did so well that the prestigious Tulane University accepted him and gave him a full scholarship through his Ph.D. in mathematics. He eventually wound up accepting Christ. After he left Tulane, he planned to work teaching school so he could save enough money to attend seminary. We were then able to bring him on our staff and have him start seminary.

This powerful, passionate preacher once told me, "Pastor Bob, I will die with you. I will go with you to my country and preach with you and serve with you."

I smiled and told him, "No Phuc, you must not die with me. I am storming the beach ahead of you. Let me get as far up on the shore as I can. If I fall, I will fall on the barbed wire fence before I die so you can climb on my back to advance. You must not stop in your native land. Don't die with me, die like me."

In his beautiful broken English, he said to me, "Okay, Pastor Bob, I will do it."

Are you ready to stop having church and *be* the church? Are you ready to see people transformed, not just converted? Are you ready to be known more for who you are and how you love than the show you put on Sunday morning? Are you ready to be the church beyond Sunday? Do you want to see your community transformed because of your church and not the community ignoring your church as irrelevant? Do you want to see your church thrive, grow, and plant other churches? Are you a young David in your heart, ready to stand before Goliath (even if you're shaking in your sandals) because you know you want to be more than what you are? Then leave your stiff armor of tradition behind, get yourself free so you can stretch out, put on your running shoes, grab your MP3, and get your game on. I'll be out there running with you.

QUESTIONS TO THINK ABOUT AND TALK ABOUT

1. Is there a unique people group in your area or an unusual person in your church from another part of the world to whom you could minister?

2. What is the primary vocation of the largest number of your church members, and how could you use that in a nation?

3. Who would be willing to take an exploratory trip to find out about that nation?

4. The biggest obstacle to keep your church from this would be_____. Explain.

APPENDIXES

For additional resources related to glocal transformation, please visit www.glocal.net.

glocalnet

Networking leaders. Advancing transformation.

www.glocal.net.

Appendix 1
Glenn Smith

PROFILE QUALITIES
FOR CHURCH PLANTERS

Essential Qualities: To what degree are the following statements true about you?

SPIRITUAL VITALITY

❑ I have frequent times that I feel exceptionally close to God.

❑ I practice spiritual disciplines and find them meaningful.

❑ I experience answered prayer and have obvious evidence of God's power in ministry.

❑ I have Scripture deeply embedded in my thinking.

❑ I exercise faith and have great confidence in God.

PERSONAL MASTERY

❑ I am highly aware of personal strengths and weaknesses.

❑ I am highly aware of how I am perceived by others.

❑ I demonstrate a high level of self-confidence without arrogance.

❑ I respond well to constructive criticism.

❑ I freely affirm others.

❑ Others think of me as a positive person.

MARRIAGE AND FAMILY READINESS

❑ My spouse and I communicate openly and warmly with each other.

❑ I provide love and discipline to my children.

❑ I balance ministry and family well.

❑ My spouse and I have created a workable partnership where we agree on time priorities as well as each partner's role and involvement in ministry.

❑ I provide a good example for other families.

❑ I handle money very well.

❑ I have strong spousal support in ministry.

CLARITY OF CALLING

❑ I have had some personal and/or ministry experiences that have led me to believe that God is preparing me and/or calling me to start a church.

❑ I have a sense from my personal time with God that he is leading me in this direction.

❑ I have received confirmation from others that this could be God's direction for me.

Starting Skills: To what degree are the following statements true about you?

RELATIONSHIP BUILDING

❑ I regularly take the initiative in getting to know new people.

❑ I am comfortable in diverse settings with diverse types of people.

❑ I have good conversational skills.

❑ I demonstrate exceptional listening skills.

❏ I make others feel secure and comfortable in my presence.

❏ I project concern for and acceptance of others.

❏ I do not respond judgmentally or prejudicially to others.

❏ I develop and maintain long-term relationships; I am an effective team builder.

PERSONAL EVANGELISM

❏ I have a deep passion for sharing the gospel with unreached people.

❏ I have identified several target groups of unreached people.

❏ I have many intentional relationships with nonbelievers.

❏ I have the ability to develop rapport with people who are far from God.

❏ I seek to identify ways to communicate the love and grace of Jesus with unreached people.

❏ I have shown unusual ability to lead people to faith in Christ.

CONTEXTUALIZATION SKILLS

❏ I study the behaviors and attitudes of people in order to know how to best relate to them.

❏ I analyze and interpret the culture accurately (I can effectively exegete culture).

❏ I am able to relate well within the culture I'm trying to reach (i.e., communication style, relational style, worship style, etc.).

❏ I am able to take biblical truth and contextualize it to my cultural target group.

❏ I am able to adapt my ministry methods to fit the context without syncretism.

❏ I understand contextual influences on my theology.

ENTREPRENEURIAL LEADERSHIP

❑ I have successfully started new ministries, businesses, programs, or ventures from scratch.

❑ I am capable in planning, organizing, and problem solving.

❑ I can gather and mobilize resources.

❑ I seek out new opportunities.

❑ I project energy and enthusiasm for new things.

❑ I have a good working knowledge about church multiplication.

Sustaining Skills: To what degree are the following statements true about you?

ENTREPRENEURIAL RESILIENCE

❑ I have demonstrated great perseverance in past ventures and have risen above adversity.

❑ I am optimistic and have a high degree of determination.

❑ I demonstrate a strong will when appropriate.

❑ I am able to stay the course with low anxiety even when challenged or attacked.

❑ I have accomplished significant things with limited resources.

DISCIPLE-MAKING SKILLS

❑ I measure success in ministry by the transformation that takes place in the lives of people.

❑ I follow up new Christians very well.

❑ I am intentional about helping believers set goals for their spiritual development.

❑ I currently have relationships where I am discipling others one-on-one or in a small group.

❑ I have a clear plan and system for discipling others that is easily transferable.

❑ I have seen many people whom I've discipled reproduce and disciple others.

LEADERSHIP DEVELOPMENT SKILLS

❑ I have developed people such that they have become effective in building relationships with people who are far from God, sharing their faith, and leading others in their spiritual journey.

❑ I regularly work with believers to help them discover their spiritual gifts and develop their skills in ministries where their gifts can flourish.

❑ I have a clear plan and reproducible system for leadership development.

❑ I delegate extensively and effectively.

❑ I have seen many people whom I've trained lead others.

FUTURING SKILLS

❑ I adapt to change readily and easily; I read and think about the future.

❑ I seek to anticipate strategic societal shifts and cultural changes.

❑ I envision what things will look like as the kingdom of God becomes visible in future cultural settings.

❑ I am effective at helping others anticipate cultural changes and I prepare them to embrace change.

❑ I continually look for pockets of unreached people.

Appendix 2
Glenn Smith

CLARIFYING YOUR CALLING

1. Describe your personality preferences/strengths, and your behavioral tendencies (Meyers-Briggs Type Indicator or the DiSC Instrument may be helpful).

2. What are the values that really motivate you?

3. Identify life verses that have shaped who you are.

4. Where did your desire to start a church come from? How has this desire been nurtured over time? Are there key people who have shaped this desire? What are the key circumstances and life experiences that have brought you to this point?

5. What are the specific objections (other churches, people) and barriers (other circumstances) you anticipate facing?

6. Who are the people who have affirmed your call to start a church?

Appendix 3
Glenn Smith

WHAT HAPPENS WHEN WE CAPTURE JESUS' VISION FOR THE KINGDOM AND START KINGDOM CHURCHES?

Our priorities change.

1. **Changed lives** becomes a priority!

Kingdom churches are no longer satisfied with just making good church members; they want to make transformational disciples who are truly "salt" and "light" in their world. Kingdom churches measure success differently.

2. **Starting new churches** becomes a priority!

Kingdom churches are reproducing churches. They are not "threatened" by new churches but want to see their city and the world saturated with vibrant new churches. They take initiative to start new churches.

3. **Community transformation** becomes a priority!

Kingdom churches have a transformational impact in their local communities. They mobilize their people to bless the community.

4. **Global impact** becomes a priority!

Kingdom churches have a transformational impact on the world. They embrace a "glocal" focus. They mobilize the church to be the missionary.

5. **United prayer** becomes a priority!

Kingdom churches and their leaders join with others in the body of Christ to pray for the transformation of their neighborhoods, their cities, and the world.

ENDNOTES

Part 1

1. For network information and resources for a model of glocal transformation, visit www.glocal.net.
2. George Barna, *Think Like Jesus* (Nashville: Integrity, 2003).

Chapter 1: How Do We Find Our Voice Again?

1. Dallas Willard, *Divine Conspiracy* (New York: HarperSanFrancisco, 1998).
2. Rick McKinley, *Jesus in the Margins* (Portland, OR: Multnomah, 2005).
3. Richard Foster, *Celebration of Discipline* (New York: HarperSanFrancisco, 1988).
4. Robert Lewis, *The Church of Irresistible Influence* (Grand Rapids: Zondervan, 2001).

Chapter 2: Where Does the Church Fit?

1. Mother Teresa, *A Simple Path* (New York: Ballantine, 1995), xxvii.
2. Stewart Brand, *The Clock of the Long Now: Time and Responsibility* (New York: Basic Books, 2000).
3. Ibid.
4. Edward Gibbon, *The Decline and Fall of the Roman Empire* (New York: Everyman's Library, 1993).
5. Stewart Brand, *The Clock of the Long Now: Time and Responsibility* (New York: Basic Books, 2000), 156.

Part 2

Chapter 4: When Will Jesus Be Enough?

1. G. K. Chesterton, *Orthodoxy* (Harrison, N.Y.: Ignatius, reprint 1995). This quote has become one of Chesterton's most notable quotes and is available on numerous websites.
2. Hudson Taylor, *Hudson Taylor's Spiritual Secret* (Chicago: Moody Press, 1954), 152.
3. Gordon MacDonald, *A Resilient Life* (Nashville: Nelson, 2005), 20.
4. Richard Foster, *Celebration of Discipline*, 1.
5. Søren Kierkegaard, *For Self-Examination: Recommended for the Times*, trans. Edna and Howard Hong (Minneapolis: Augsburg, 1940), 66–67.

6. E. Stanley Jones, *Mastery: The Art of Mastering Life* (Nashville: Abingdon, reprint 1991).

Chapter 5: Can Following Jesus Ever Be Private?

1. Jon R. Katzenbach and Douglas K. Smith, *The Wisdom of Teams* (New York: HarperBusiness, 2003).

Part 3

1. I learned and developed the concept of domain jumping from reading *Good Work: When Excellence and Ethics Meet*, by Howard Gardner (New York: Basic Books, 2002), and *Geeks and Geezers*, by Warren Bennis (Boston: Harvard Business School Press, 2002).

Chapter 7: What Would It Look Like for the Church to Turn the World Upside Down?

1. Bosch, Guder, Van Gelder, and others have written on this, but thus far it has been primarily theory. This is what we want to practice.

Chapter 8: Do We Want to Be the Biggest Church in the Area, or Church the Area?

1. Dr. Roy Fish, class lecture, Southwestern Seminary, 1982.

SUBJECT INDEX

We want to hear from you. Please send your comments about this book to us in care of zreview@zondervan.com. Thank you.

Share Your Thoughts

With the Author: Your comments will be forwarded to the author when you send them to *zauthor@zondervan.com*.

With Zondervan: Submit your review of this book by writing to *zreview@zondervan.com*.

Free Online Resources at
www.zondervan.com

Zondervan AuthorTracker: Be notified whenever your favorite authors publish new books, go on tour, or post an update about what's happening in their lives at www.zondervan.com/authortracker.

Daily Bible Verses and Devotions: Enrich your life with daily Bible verses or devotions that help you start every morning focused on God. Visit www.zondervan.com/newsletters.

Free Email Publications: Sign up for newsletters on Christian living, academic resources, church ministry, fiction, children's resources, and more. Visit www.zondervan.com/newsletters.

Zondervan Bible Search: Find and compare Bible passages in a variety of translations at www.zondervanbiblesearch.com.

Other Benefits: Register yourself to receive online benefits like coupons and special offers, or to participate in research.

ZONDERVAN®

ZONDERVAN.com/
AUTHORTRACKER
follow your favorite authors